MONE

YOUR BOOK

with a

COURSE

Your Guide to Quickly Creating a Profitable and Impactful Course from Your Book

LUCAS MARINO

MONETIZE YOUR BOOK

WITH A

COURSE

Your Guide to Quickly Creating a Profitable and Impactful Course from Your Book

LUCAS MARINO

ISBN Hardcover: 978-1-960535-02-3

ISBN Paperback: 978-1-960535-01-6

ISBN eBook: 978-1-960535-00-9

TABLE OF CONTENTS

SPECIAL INVITATION

I'd like to personally invite you to download the book bonuses and more!

Just visit: https://www.marinotraining.com/pages/book-offers

FOREWORD
BY HONORÉE CORDER

Have you ever met someone and been immediately struck by how likeable, nice, *and* smart they were—in the same five minutes? That's my experience with Lucas Marino.

Lucas and I met when he took one of my courses, and he attended the live Q&A sessions. He asked great questions, was beyond respectful, and always offered to help the other students when he could. He's the consummate professional, and an all-around great human. Even though he's retired from the military, has a doctorate, and has been in business now for several years, he is always humble, open, and ready to laugh.

Lucas is just the kind of person I like to know and have as a friend, as well as work with. Taking a course was first, then he joined my mastermind, and next came the opportunity to partner in a business venture. These different situations have given me rare insight into Lucas, his personality, and his abilities.

Lucky for me—and you—he's extremely knowledgeable when it comes to creating online content and courses. He knows courses and course platforms in a way few others do. And he knows how to help people turn their knowledge and expertise into courses. The best news of all is he's put it all down in this book, and you're just pages away from knowing exactly how to, yes, *monetize your book with a course.*

Even though I've created several courses, some by myself and some with a lot of help, I didn't know what I still didn't know. Turns out that what I didn't know was limiting my impact, as well as costing me time and money. While that was a bummer to realize, I am armed with a level of knowledge that is now available to you, too!

You've done the hard work of writing a book. This book is going to not only inspire you to turn the expertise you included in your book into a course in the fastest, easiest, and most effective way possible; it's going to give you what you need to know, when you need to know it, so your courses will reach the right students at the right time and in just the right way. All while you add an income stream to your business.

Pretty cool, right?

Not only that, but you'll feel like Lucas is right there with you, answering your questions (sometimes before you have them, other times in the very next paragraph). You've got a friend, someone who really cares about you, as you outline your course, decide whether to do a video or handout, and finally get to the moment when you hit the "publish!" button.

One more thing: I didn't create new courses for several years because I was intimidated. It felt to me like it was easier to do it wrong and fail than it was to do it right and succeed. Turns out, I had it all backwards. With the right guidance and support, you can create a course based on your book in a fraction of the time it took to write your book! So, dig in and learn what you need to learn. Then get to some serious course creating!

Honorée Corder
Author, *You Must Write a Book* & *You Must Market Your Book*

INTRODUCTION

Welcome, creators!

I am excited that you have picked up this book, and not just because you bought it. *Thank you for that.*

I'm excited because you and I have a lot in common, and I love sharing my experience in developing courses and online training businesses with other professionals like you.

You see, it wasn't so long ago that I was in your exact seat. I was an aspiring business owner, a solopreneur, and a subject matter expert, looking for a way to share my expertise with others. What if I could build a business doing exactly that?

Maybe I could make enough money to leave my full-time job as an engineer.

One reason I wanted to become an entrepreneur was because I had the desire to be the master of my destiny. It had nothing to do with the pay. I was making plenty of money working on military projects, and I had a position that filled my cup every day. The work was enjoyable, and I enjoyed the people I worked with; things were fantastic.

Still, I had this *urge* to do something else.

What is your vision? Maybe you want to leave your full-time grind, too. Or is there something else driving you? Understanding your "why" is the first step toward living your dream.

So, let's talk about your "why" for a moment.

Whatever your reason, you've been inspired to do something unique. You are, or were, motivated to start your own business and serve others.

Starting a business and training people can be exciting and rewarding.

You may go into business for yourself because you are an expert in something and want to share your expertise with others.

Perhaps you currently own a business and see training people in your area of expertise as a profitable way to expand your product line.

Maybe you're a content creator looking for a new way to leverage your content for revenue. Or maybe you're starting a business because you've recently had a significant professional life event, like retirement or a job loss.

Are you now looking for ways to create products that can help other people when you can't depend on a company for income?

Maybe you want some additional income while you enjoy retirement, or to put some money away earlier in your career for later in life.

Clearly, there are many worthy reasons to start a content-based business.

You might have many answers to the question of "why," but some of them are going to hit a little closer to your heart than others.

For me, it was a return to the fire and passion I'd felt when I dreamed of becoming a writer or musician in my youth. Back then, pursuing a creative career wasn't practical. So, I put my dreams on hold and joined the Coast Guard. It was after I retired from the military that I saw there was an opportunity to become what I originally felt I would be as a creator.

Your reason (your "why") for wanting to become a creative entrepreneur may be very different from mine. But it is important—whatever it is.

While thinking about your reason(s) for wanting to start your business, you also want to consider the longevity and structure of your training business line. Maybe your plan is to sell it and cash in when it matures into a respectable business. Or will you create and nurture your business for a lifetime?

Both are perfectly fine.

You may be the person who wants to partner with someone else in your training business. Or maybe you prefer to fly solo.

As you can see, there are many things to consider when becoming an entrepreneur and starting a training business.

Regardless of your "why," you must be all-in as an entrepreneur.

One reason I wanted to be an entrepreneur was for the flexibility and excitement that entrepreneurship provides. I love exploring new ways to do things, innovative ways of thinking, new ways of serving others, and the outright joy of creating something from nothing.

All of that is highly attractive to me, and entrepreneurship provides that type of experience in an almost-aggressive fashion. You are always *all-in* on creative activity. If that terrifies you, this isn't the gig for you.

But if that excites you, what are you waiting for?

CHAPTER ONE:

A BIT OF MOTIVATION

Regardless of your reason for creating a course from your book or launching a training business within an existing business, I hope you'll understand a few key things.

First, *you can absolutely do this.* There's nothing impossible about the work ahead of you. Nothing!

Second, you have no reason *not* to have fun building courses or a training business line. You will meet remarkable people and create engaging, worthwhile, and valuable content. You're going to do amazing things for other people. All of that has a high potential for being fun.

Third, you're not alone. There are tons of content creators: subject-matter experts, coaches, authors, artists, and various other professionals. These people have created training programs and done well in their businesses by doing so.

You are not the first person to venture down this path. You will not be the last.

More good news: Never have there been more tools available, more support resources, and more people who naturally respect small business and entrepreneurship and are willing to invest in training products. You can capitalize on building in a time of high demand and familiarization.

Did I mention you can absolutely do this?

There isn't a magic pill that you can take to make it all happen—it will take work.

*The good news is that **I'm going to share the lessons, observations, insights, emotions, successes, and failures I experienced** during the five years I spent building my business from nothing to something that provides income for my family and others.*

And there is a lot to share; some things you will learn on the following pages include:

- How your published book can set you up perfectly for creating a course
- How to identify the goals and objectives of your course
- How to develop your curriculum and select your lesson types
- Online training and course creation on a learning management system (LMS)
- Technology and the tools available to the course creator
- Pricing options for your course—making money
- Conceptualizing minicourses and course bundles
- Customer relationship management software (CRM)
- Course sales considerations

Just to name a few.

When you've finished studying this content, you will have access to the tools and information you need to create your course from start to finish. But take your time because there is a significant amount of information to take in.

Be patient with yourself during the process while also possessing an insatiable hunger that's not easily satisfied. You're hungry!

At every turn, you are growing and experiencing new things. You don't do it because you must, but because it's a BIG part of you. One reason you're doing it is that you're addicted to adventure and growth. You're excited about the potential and really want to get at it!

REGARDLESS OF YOUR POSITION IN LIFE AND BUSINESS, THAT HUNGER, THAT DESIRE, THE ADVENTURE, SHOULD BE THERE.

I'm not saying you're going to wake up hyper-motivated every day. There will be days when you wake up tired and go to sleep exhausted or frustrated. You may be weary of some obstacle or challenge that you can't seem to overcome (at least, for the moment). That's all part of the experience—the adventure.

Regardless of how your day started or ended, when your head crashes into your pillow for the night, you can say that you're doing something that many people are afraid of or hesitant to take on. You'll also be able to say that you created something that helps people and will provide for you as much as it will provide for others.

You can support your family. It is possible to support other people's families. It is possible for you to provide yourself with new freedoms. You can do all these things. And you can be proud of that.

You are one step closer to that freedom, or you're already there and enjoy being there. Whichever phase of that lifecycle you're in, know that you are making progress.

And that's a blessing!

If this resonates with you, congratulations, you're reading a book that you will relate to. Hopefully, you'll benefit from the recommendations and advice in these pages. Most importantly, you'll share your gift with the world with more intention because you invested time in learning more about something you're passionate about.

Are you ready?

YOU PUBLISHED A BOOK; YOU CAN PUBLISH A COURSE

The similarities between developing and publishing a nonfiction book and publishing a course are too good to be true. The logic and processes involved make them natural companions.

You were likely motivated to write a book to share your knowledge with people who could benefit from your expertise. You may have also seen the potential for your book to produce financial benefits such as royalties (traditional publishing) or book sales profit (independent publishing).

Perhaps you wanted to establish a reputation in your industry. Perhaps you did it to leave a legacy that will outlive you. You created a piece of literature that has the potential to make a lasting impression on others long after you depart this life. That's wild stuff!

Courses present many of the same benefits.

As nice as all of that is, the similarities between the products and processes are probably more relevant to you, as a reader of this book.

You wrote your book in a logical flow of ideas to educate or inform your readers: an outline. Courses also have an outline based on a logical flow of information.

You selected an attractive cover for your book, labored over the fonts and images, and decided on all the pleasant words on the front and back covers. That title took some thought! All the things that help a person who sees your book for the first time understand the topic and why they should read it. Courses have these things as well! We call them landing pages and course cards. Every course has a front and back cover in the form of a landing page.

And every course has a course card or thumbnail image that represents it. When people see the course card image on a button, a banner, or some type of promotional information, they can associate the picture with your course.

Your book cover should attract me to your book. It must grab my attention! Your landing page and course card should create the same experience. The images and copy represent your course and convince your potential learner to explore the course further.

Now, when they look at the back cover, things get deeper. The information flows. The same thing happens to potential learners when they see your course landing page. They read the details of the curriculum and how your course will help them. They see enough detail to inspire them to enroll.

Okay, so we've got some similarities to a book's exterior nailed down.

- Title
- Cover art in the form of a course image and landing page
- Back cover and jacket copy in the form of landing page copy
- The course image is attractive

Completely logical so far, right? Right! Let's explore some similarities in creating the content.

When you wrote your book, you logically created the flow of the information. You may have asked yourself, "What exactly do I want this reader to learn? In what order do I want to present the information to them?"

You're going to do the same thing with your course. In fact, whenever an author comes to me to develop a course, I first ask to see their book's outline or table of contents. They've already organized their topic in a logical flow. I'm going to see a similar logic path in their course outline. I will gain a basic understanding of what they teach and the order in which they present the material based on the book's table of contents.

It isn't automatically assumed to teach the exact flow of the book or to cover the entire table of contents from the book in the course. Nor does it mean the course will reflect the exact content of the book. By the time we're done, we may add content; we may remove content. You could develop an entire course based on a single chapter from the book.

The reason for this is, most times, the book serves a different purpose than the course, though this isn't always the case. Sometimes the book and the course serve the same purpose, and using the table of contents from the book as the course outline is completely logical. As we create the curriculum, we trim, add, or move things around. We aren't constrained by the book's content; we are building a separate product here.

Time has passed since you wrote the book, and you've discovered new things, methods, processes, information, and case studies. You may want to share new information or lessons that weren't available or included in the book.

So, the book and course may not automatically mirror each other, but the flow of the information derived from the book's outline may be very similar.

You may be curious about how to decide whether to deviate from using the same outline or table of contents from the book to serve the same purpose for the course.

Well, it truly depends on what you want your course to do for its learners. What outcome(s) do you want the learner to achieve after successfully completing the course?

That's the million-dollar question.

Your learner picks up your book to get information and learn about a topic, or to learn how to do something related to that topic. You, as the author, relay that information to them in the written words in your book. Well, the course opens an entirely new world of content delivery.

We will break down these content options in future chapters, but I'll give you a quick rundown here.

Books are powerful and beautiful. However, they limit you to using only words and images (audiobooks being the exception, of course). You may have a workbook that brings a learner closer to the topic by making them apply their knowledge, think through problems, and write out their answers. A workbook can guide them through a process or prompt thought patterns to move them from learning to action.

Your course can do this same thing or meet these same goals in more dynamic ways.

For example, you can write text, host a video, or have audio over images. Digital pictures, animations, and games are possible. Downloads, PDFs, and templates are available content. You can use interactive quizzes and post surveys. You can even post video-based quizzes and allow your learner to interact with a video. They can select options and answers from the video screen that take them to other videos made specifically for people who choose those answers. Cool, right?

These are examples of elements that you can include in a course. You can see how these may change your outline.

You now have new tools in your toolbox to deliver information! They may change the way you deliver information to the learner and alter the logical flow of the content. You may add or remove lessons based on the topic and how you want to communicate it to your learner.

If you've designed your course to help a learner close a performance gap, then your aim is not simply to be an outstanding source of information. An encyclopedia is an outstanding source of information, but it does not teach you how to do things.

If you want to close gaps in performance and help somebody do something new or better, you want to focus on closing those gaps.

This is where quizzes, surveys, games, or workbooks can come in handy. You're helping someone apply their thinking, but ultimately, you're helping them close a performance gap. So, your content needs to be geared specifically toward that end. You don't want to overwhelm the learner with unnecessary information. (We'll talk about this more in the section on goals and objectives.)

Again, you can see how these considerations may change the face of your table of contents.

Do you see the similarities between books and courses?

We've talked about covers, what information to include, and about the need for an outline.

We've talked about the purpose of your book, and why you wrote it. Let's move to the similarities in your experiences.

As the book's author and course's host, you created both products with intended outcomes for a reader or learner. You experienced the writing and the production of the book—the creation of every word—the assembly of logical thoughts, one preceding the other into engaging content. You've also worked with other professionals to produce that book: editors, copywriters, and publishers. This is very similar to your course.

You're going to interact with other people and start with nothing to create something great. You will refine your content over time and produce a quality product for consumption by a human you've never met. They have clearly defined needs, and you have a well-produced product to help meet their needs.

You went through a process to create that book, choosing every element. When writing your book, you chose imagery and wrote every word. You'll do the same when creating your course. You have experience! Be overjoyed; you are on familiar land!

I want you to see that you really know where to start—you know what to do. In fact, you're more prepared to do this than you know. With the right tools in your toolbox, and a little direction, you'll create your course. It's going to feel like riding a bike.

CHAPTER TWO:

DEVELOP YOUR CURRICULUM

You have expertise that you want to share with others. You have options to do this via a myriad of formats and delivery methods, all of which can be helpful to an audience.

Content creators communicate with their audience through their products. Books are one avenue, and courses are another. Many content creators also communicate through coaching programs, webinars, blogs, podcasts, or consulting programs. These products offer viable opportunities for your business to prosper while delivering products to customers in a meaningful and valuable way.

Think of each of them as a means of communication. Some people want to be communicated to in a certain way, by a certain medium. By sharing your expertise across these multiple product types, you may reach different people (i.e., learners, readers, or clients).

You can communicate your message in a new and exciting way.

You may be an author trying to figure out how to expand the reach of your written work or capitalize on the power, strength, and authority of your book in a new and lucrative way. Courses are a fantastic way to do so.

The content and experience of a course is referred to as a curriculum. Every lesson you deliver and every exercise or assessment the learner completes is part of the curriculum.

Are you ready to learn how to develop *your* course curriculum? Let's get to it!

YOUR CURRICULUM SERVES YOUR LEARNERS

As covered in the previous chapter, you can easily consider the outline of your book as an initial outline for your course, though it doesn't have to mirror the outline of your book exactly. You may select key themes or topics from your book and list them in logical order. This list becomes your draft course curriculum. In this situation, your course does not one hundred percent reflect the outline of your book, but the core tenants of your book remain intact for the course.

Once you've done this, you can consider the content of each of those chapters as the starting point for your curriculum. It's time to ask questions to take the draft outline to the next level.

What does the end user need to see and hear?

What do they need to learn?

What is fundamental to their understanding before they move on to the next chapter or lesson?

You can ask these questions at each level of the outline. By answering these simple questions, you either confirm that the book content serves the purpose of the course, or that you need to take a different approach to the course. Perhaps your student needs to see the information differently than they can in the book. Perhaps they need more information than what you provided in the book. This is your opportunity to assemble your curriculum in a way that *serves the learner*.

YOU'LL FIND THAT THEME RESONATING THROUGHOUT THIS BOOK. YOUR CURRICULUM DOES NOT EXIST TO SERVE YOU, THE INSTRUCTOR, THE ENTREPRENEUR, OR THE CREATOR. YOUR CURRICULUM **EXISTS TO SERVE THE LEARNER/CONSUMER.**

We will use the following 5 points to organize our efforts to build a curriculum to serve the learner.

1. **Identify your ideal learner.** Your course serves the learner first, and your business second. You must know who the learner is before you take another step forward. This *may* not be the same profile as your book's ideal reader.
2. **Identify the learner's problem.** What problem does your learner need help with? You must identify the problem before you spend a second developing the solution (course). The problem may be a performance gap, needed skill, or some other deficiency that affects their life.
3. **Identify and validate the solution.** What solution do you offer to solve the learner's problem? Does it really solve their problem? Are you *sure?*
4. **Identify the learner's outcome.** When the learner solves their problem with your solution, what outcome will the learner achieve?
5. **Identify learning objectives.** The learner will complete learning objectives as they work through the curriculum. The objectives help the learner achieve the outcome.

Let's dive in!

WHO IS YOUR IDEAL LEARNER?

It is common practice in business to identify our *ideal client or customer avatar* (ICA). While your business exists to serve this ICA, your course will exist to serve an ideal learner.

This concept should be familiar. You most likely wrote your book for a specific reader. It's possible that you wrote a book for a specific person.

Approach your course with a similar goal: to serve a particular learner.

Who is this learner? Where do they live? What do they do for a living? Do they have a name or title that is easy to identify?

Maybe someone you know by name fits the description of your ideal learner! That's fantastic. Design your course exactly for that person.

It isn't the end of the world if you can't drill down to that level of detail. Just remember that the more defined the learner profile, the tighter the niche you'll serve, and, as you've probably heard, the riches are in the niches. You eliminate competition, resonate more richly with learners, and focus your message more clearly when you define the specific person you serve.

There are many ways to develop the profile for your ideal learner. One simple and familiar way is to ask Who, What, Where, When, and (of course) Why.

Who do you picture in your mind benefiting most from this course? Describe this person, including age, job, gender, hobbies—the works!

What problem do they experience that your course may solve for them? What outcome do they need from this course? What impact would this have on their job or personal life?

Where do they live and work? Where will they attend the course? Online or in-person? At home or work? Or both?

When do they experience the problem? When do they need your solution? When can they attend your course? Is it at work, at home, or on their commute?

Why do they have this problem? Why would they choose your course to solve their problem? Why would they spend their money to solve this problem?

When you consider the importance of knowing who will buy and attend your course, it is easy to appreciate the importance of identifying your ideal learner.

The ideal learner will connect with you. You will market to the ideal learner. You will serve the ideal learner through your course. And, if all goes well, you will receive repeat business and referrals from your ideal learner. As great as all of that is, the genuine joy will come when you build a relationship with your ideal learner that exceeds your expectations!

COURSE GOALS AND OBJECTIVES

Your curriculum provides the learner with the information needed to achieve the **outcomes** and **objectives** of your course.

The outcomes of a course may be generic or very specific, but they must always be *valuable* to the learner.

For example, a desired outcome may be to learn how to make a peanut butter and jelly sandwich, how to perform a business case analysis, how to paint a cat, or file taxes. These are outcomes associated with the learner's performance.

Upon successful completion of your course, what will that student be able to do? These are the outcomes.

Objectives are targets along the way to meeting the goal and producing outcomes. When aggregated, the objectives are a series of completed tasks that help the learner achieve the intended outcomes.

The "paint the cat" example may include:

1. First objective: know how to find a mildly irritated cat (this is their natural state).
2. Second objective: know how to select appropriate paints.
3. Third objective: know how to soothe your cat before painting.

4. Fourth objective: know how to run for cover. The hairy creature is not down with the paint.

RELAX… I'm being sarcastic. Of course, I would never encourage you to actually paint your cat. In fact, what I originally meant by "paint a cat" was to create a painting *of* a cat. Let's use that example.

1. First objective: understand how to select your paints.
2. Second objective: understand how to select a canvas.
3. Third objective: understand how to select the appropriate paint brushes.
4. Fourth objective: demonstrate how to stage your area for painting.

And so, the list goes, in a logical order, until the learner has completed all objectives required to achieve the stated outcomes.

Once you have the outcomes and objectives outlined, you can start thinking of what to include in each lesson. At a high level, *the key to content is to simplify complex topics into lessons that drive performance outcomes.*

Focus on what helps the learner complete the objectives and achieve outcomes. Nothing more and nothing less.

The student is there to learn for specific reasons, so we strive to eliminate anything that doesn't contribute to their decisions or action.

I encourage you to ask, "Can they succeed without this info?" If the answer is no, it goes into the curriculum; if the answer is yes, set it aside as an additional resource or eliminate it entirely.

The more technical the product, the more important it is to not overwhelm the learner with information that is not critical. Make sure you don't overload them. An overloaded learner is an unhappy learner.

If you dump every bit of topic info onto an unsuspecting learner, particularly info that doesn't directly support an objective, you may receive some spicy feedback. "This is a very complex topic that needs a simplified solution, and I was hoping to find it here. I guess not!"

The magic is in *the simple solution.*

As a subject expert, you are in the driver's seat. Take the learner on the most direct and efficient route possible. The volume of information that you dump will never measure the effectiveness of your course. It will only be measured by your learner's satisfaction. Be sure that they can put into practice what you give them.

This is the beauty and curse of being the subject matter expert!

CHAPTERS AND LESSONS

Let's talk about the building blocks of a course. Just like in your book, you will break your course into chapters. In your book, chapters contain sections as paragraphs. In your course, the chapters contain lessons.

Lessons are bite-sized chunks of your course. They are the individual segments of content that you deliver to your student. Each lesson may contain one video, audio, or presentation file and may also contain a body of text to accompany the visual or audio element.

So, the large sections of the course are called chapters, just like in your book. Each chapter contains lessons. You may have a course that is short and sweet. It could be one chapter with one lesson. Or, you could have a very comprehensive course with tons of lessons within many chapters.

The way to approach chapters and lessons is to assume that each chapter will have a common topic or theme.

Remember, when you created your curriculum, you created a logical step-by-step presentation of information. Now we're going to organize that information in a series of lessons, and we're going to group those lessons in a logical group called a chapter.

A CHAPTER IS A LOGICAL GROUPING OF ONE OR MORE LESSONS AROUND A TOPIC OR THEME.

Now, it's important to be flexible with these terms once you build your course in a learning management system, as different systems use different terms. I know, it's terribly nice of them to do that. Right?

It doesn't really matter what you call chapters and lessons. It's more important that you know *what* they are and their intended *purpose.*

So, what does this mean for you as the writer of a nonfiction book? What do you do with this?

I talked about the logical grouping of information and adapting the outline of your book to create a course outline. Look at you! You've created your logical groups of chapters and lessons.

Here is a simplified example of a basic course layout:

- Introduction (normally Chapter 1)
- Topic-related material (Chapters 2, 3, 4...)
- Final chapter to close the course
- Additional resources or extras

Okay! As you can see, this isn't terribly difficult. The first chapter is normally an introduction to the course. Chapter 1 lessons might include a course outline, an introduction video, a "how to use this course" lesson, and a quick questionnaire about the learner's experience with the topic and desired outcomes. Here is an example of an introductory chapter layout:

Chapter 1 – Welcome to the Coolest Course Ever

- Lesson 1 – A Message from (insert your name here).
    - This is a brief video telling the learner what they'll learn in this chapter and why it's important to them. Cover outcomes and objectives.
- Lesson 2 – How to use this course.
    - This lesson tells the learner how to navigate the course player and materials.
- Lesson 3 – Let's Learn More About You!

    - This is a quick survey to learn more about the learner's familiarity with the topic and their expected outcomes.
- Lesson 4 – Links.
    - If there are any live sessions, you can post the link here so students can refer to it.
    - If the students need to download a workbook or e-book, this is a great place to park it.

After the introductory chapter (normally Chapter 1), you fill the course with all the topic-related content. This is where you teach the learner all the things, and they do all the activities. Here is an example of a topic-focused chapter layout:

Chapter (2, 3, 4, ...) – Building the Coolest Book Ever

- Lesson 1 - Introduction Video.
    - This is a brief video telling the learner what they'll learn in this chapter and why it's important to them. Cover chapter outcomes and objectives.
- Lesson 2 – Presentation of material.
    - This is where you deliver the information that they need to achieve the first objective. Normally, I default to a video, but you decide whether video, audio, or text is most appropriate for the learner and material.
- Lesson 3 – Application/exercise.
    - This is where the learning meets action! You can present the learner with a worksheet, workbook, or other practical exercises. This lesson should help the learner put their new knowledge to work toward meeting an objective.
- Lesson 4 – Assessment.
    - This is where you test the learner's recall and grasp of the material through a quiz, survey, or test.

- Lesson 5 – Additional Resources.
  - Deliver any additional resources of value related to the chapter. These could include downloadable PDFs, links, or other references.
  - This is a great opportunity to introduce the learner to your book! Drop a recommendation like, "You can learn more about this topic in Chapter X of my book titled, *The Best Book Ever*. Here's the link."

After you've delivered all the course materials needed to meet all course objectives, you will close the course with a final chapter. The closing chapter is important because it reinforces everything that they learned and provides them with guidance for "what's next."

The simplest way to approach the reinforcement is through this ridiculous but memorable phrase.

TELL THEM WHAT YOU TOLD THEM.

Easy, right? Before you panic, don't worry, you aren't going to rehash the entire course. You will cover the high points and recap the big takeaways. No deep dives here, folks.

Next, you can point them toward the next steps in their journey. This may be the first course in a series of courses on a topic, and you can point them to the next course. Or this may be a standalone course with no follow-on courses. In that case, you'll want to close in a way that allows the student to stand on their own afterward by sharing your contact information and additional resources.

I recommend placing an "Additional Resources" chapter after the course closes. This information isn't necessary for completing the course but gives the learner more information, references, and products to help them as they move to put their knowledge into practice. You can recommend books, courses, articles, blogs, organizations, websites, and other professionals.

I also include the downloads scattered throughout the course in one "Downloads" chapter. This is very helpful for learners who can't remember the specific chapter that contained that one helpful PDF or spreadsheet that they need. Having all downloads available in one easy-to-find location is super helpful.

As you can see, courses are groups of one or more chapters. Chapters are groups of one or more lessons. Lessons contain the information that the student needs to succeed in the course. And the flow of these chapters and their lessons is based on the logical flow of your course outline.

When you step back and look at it, everything is organized and logical.

ASSESSMENTS - QUIZZES, SURVEYS, TESTS, AND EXAMS

It's everyone's favorite topic—assessments! Don't panic; you aren't being assessed here. There won't be a pop quiz, a test, or an anonymous survey waiting for you at the end of this chapter.

Assessments are an instructor's way of measuring learner performance against the course objectives. In plain language, assessments help you know if they are learning the course materials.

If the objective of a lesson is to "understand" or "know" something, you may use a quiz to determine if the learner can correctly recall what you taught them. Let's look at a basic example:

Objective: The learner will know how many pieces of bread they need to make a peanut butter and jelly sandwich.

Sample Quiz Question: How many slices of bread do you need to make a single peanut butter and jelly sandwich?

Sample Options:

A. 1-slice of bread

B. 2-slices of bread

C. 3-slices of bread

D. 5-slices of bread

As you can see, we have a course objective addressed in a lesson. Upon completion of that lesson, we may quiz the learner to determine their recall of the material.

We aren't doing this to torture the learner. (Who wants a quiz?) Assessing recall is an effective way of ensuring the learner understands the delivered course material and can apply their new knowledge. In the end, we need them to apply knowledge if we want them to achieve outcomes.

So, why use a quiz? Use a quiz to assess recall. When building a quiz, you can assess recall using multiple-choice, true or false, or fill-in-the-blank questions.

What if we want to build a long quiz? Well, that would be a test. That's right, a test is a long quiz. Simple, right? If you ask more than a dozen questions and cover a lot of material, you are venturing into the land of testing. Typically, tests carry more weight than a quiz as well. For example, quizzes may be worth 20-30 percent of your grade, but tests may be worth much more. Since quizzes ask fewer questions and cover less material, they usually carry less weight in the final grade.

Why use a survey? Use a survey to get input or feedback from a student regarding the course material minus criteria that includes right or wrong answers.

For example, a learner may complete a lesson, and rather than assess them for right or wrong answers to a question, you may be interested in their interpretation of the topic. Or you may encourage them to list all the ways they can apply the lesson to their work. There is no right or wrong answer in those two scenarios, so a survey is an option.

What about exams? Exams are formal, carry significant weight in the final grade, and may be grounds for achieving a specified result. For example, you may attend a course to learn project management and prepare for a project management certification exam. Eventually, you complete the course, but you aren't certified until you pass the certification exam. Congratulations on your education! To become certified, you must complete this rigorous, proctored exam with a passing grade of 80% or better. Exams are normally "owned" or hosted by an organization that issues a credential of some sort. This isn't always the case, but it is very popular.

In academic settings, the exam may be the last test in the course and may require a minimum passing grade for the learner to satisfy course requirements. Never mind if the learner aced all the quizzes and classwork, they must also achieve a minimum passing grade on the exam. Welcome to exams!

For the sake of your course, having quizzes or surveys is normal. Testing would be the next level. Exams would be outside of the norm for an online course hosted by an entrepreneur who does not issue a professional certification.

SCRIPT WRITING OR NAH?

Authors creating courses often ask me whether or not they should write scripts for their video lessons. The answer depends on you, the speaker, the creator, the instructor.

If you are creating audio files (no video, just audio), scripts are a great idea. If you can read a script naturally without sounding like a robot, using a script for an audio lesson is a fantastic approach.

Video is trickier. If you choose to use scripts for video, consider using a teleprompter. A teleprompter or teleprompter app prevents you from flipping or holding pages or reaching out every 20 seconds while you read to move a sheet or note on your desk.

If you don't want to read a script during your video lesson, you may choose to use one as a primer for your brain. For example, you can read the script several times before filming your video to drill the key points and flow of words into your memory. Then, you can use a list of the bullet points close at hand while recording to guide you while you record your video. Consider this a guide for your thinking, use short-term memory to your advantage, and keep the "live" feel by not reading directly from a script while recording. I do this often! I put together bullet points and post them next to my camera so that I don't have to look down while recording, then rock and roll.

Regardless of whether you read from a script or choose to only use notes, you'll most likely record multiple takes. Don't beat yourself up if it takes several attempts to make a short video. That's just part of the game. It's the nature of video. Just like when you wrote your book, and it took several passes by you and your editor to progress from a rough draft to a real draft. Remember that?

So, let's say you decide to write a script for a video. The good news is that you do not need to write it like a book. Don't be so formal. Be conversational yet clean and make sure the script flows naturally. If you are a technical writer, like I was, writing scripts can be challenging. Try to loosen up. Focus on natural language and pace.

Reading a script without sounding like you're reading a script may be challenging and a special skill. One of my clients started his career on television and radio. It was so much fun writing scripts and handing them to him because I couldn't wait to hear what came back. The videos looked like a morning television show, and the audio files sounded exactly like an audiobook or a radio broadcast, minus the cheesy radio voice, of course. He understood how to pace his words and how to use voice inflection.

You are on the hook to educate and entertain. Your audience can quickly lose focus on your lesson if you bore them by awkwardly reading, if you're nervous and flat, distracting, or if you do not make eye contact with the camera.

Now, I will not sit here and lecture writers about how to write a script. You know what works best for your writing style. If you struggle to keep the natural flow of speech and natural word selection, you can keep things as close to speech as possible by using a transcription app like Otter.ai to record yourself speaking and transcribe your words. When you're done recording your speaking session, go through the transcript, clean up the loose words and errors, and call it good. Congratulations, you have your draft script.

Another option is to use a section of your book to create a lesson. Again, make it sound a bit more conversational and use that as the foundation for your content.

RECORDING VIDEO

We're here! Recording video and audio for lessons is where the magic happens. (I've been dying to say that.) Video and audio content brings so much life to a course and truly differentiates your book from your course. This isn't an audiobook version of your print book. We're here to do much more than that!

Because video and audio can be so different from the printed word, many authors worry about making these lessons. Not you. Not anymore!

Let's start with video.

Video is king. Without a doubt, the most important lesson format is video. Video is dynamic and, in reasonably priced courses, expected. Video provides streams of your teaching, animations, and presentations. Whether live or recorded, video gives the student a way to see you, hear you, and see what they're learning. Video brings you and the students together.

Videos are great for lectures, demonstrations, and the visual presentation of data and information. Your book may have contained visual content like charts, tables, pictures, and more. Want to present those visuals in your course? Video can do that.

You're not limited to only printing a chart in a text file or in a PDF. You can build these visuals into a presentation (e.g., PowerPoint, Canva) and then make a video out of it. Or you can embed these elements directly into post-video editing and make it look as if the data is on the screen with you.

Shoot, you can even create an animation using software like Powtoon and really get creative! In the end, you have a video file in hand and a lot of creative options.

Let's talk about the basics of making video. The first thing you must do is decide whether video is the best way for you to present the material.

I can hear you now. "Wait, what? Didn't you just spend several paragraphs telling me that video is the best way to present material? What gives, dude?"

Video is the best way to present *most* material, but there is some discretion to be had. After all, it wouldn't make sense to make video of a quiz, would it?

What are you trying to do? Present information or test the learner's recall? For presentations, video is fantastic. For recalling information, you'd choose a quiz.

Since you are building an on-demand course or a hybrid course (a mix of recorded and live sessions viewed over the internet), video will be great for instructional content.

You also want to be as engaging as possible. Video is usually better in this case than audio or text alone.

You've made your mind up. You are making a video.

The first thing you do is assemble your material. You whip up a lesson outline based on the content of a chapter of your book that covers the topic. That helps a lot! You read the chapter of your book several times to re-familiarize yourself with the details, the flow of information, and the main points. Rock and roll!

You jot the highlights down in order on a series of sticky notes and put them on your computer monitor directly under your webcam (see what we're doing here? Your eyes will be very close to your webcam when you scan the notes).

It's time to take care of the visual elements of the video. Are you a disheveled mess, or did you wake up perfect (again)? Need to change clothes (don't panic, pajama bottoms are good if they are out of view)? Need to shave, do your hair, fix your makeup?

Let's get your scene's background squared away. If you are shooting a video without a presentation, your background will be very important. Don't over-analyze the background elements, keep this simple. Focus on making it clean, controlling the sound and light, and removing distractions.

(We love live animals, but they don't belong in your background unless your course is about those animals.)

You don't want to hear the neighbor's lawnmower, your kid's television, or your family's conversation. You don't want a bright window or a random door behind you. You don't want adjacent rooms in clear view where you expect foot traffic.

You also don't want a poorly controlled virtual background where the filming software struggles to separate you from the background, and you look like you are under attack from some crazy fuzz from outer space that feeds on the head and shoulders of unsuspecting teachers. You know what I'm talking about.

We've all been in virtual meetings where an attendee used a virtual background, and their image is constantly struggling to separate them from the background. It's distracting. If you are going to use a virtual background, use a green screen to improve the image.

So, what do you want? Balanced or accent light is good. Bookshelves, houseplants, attractive colors, or a plain background are all good. Just avoid distractions and make sure the professionalism of the scene matches that of your course.

Can you take the video outside of the typical office view? Of course! Filming in nature is fine. Filming on a stage is normally fine as well. You can film in any scene you like if it doesn't distract the learner or pose too much contrast to the topic. For example, filming a lesson on book editing in a local cardboard manufacturing plant wouldn't make much sense, would it? Yes, the plant is cool, but it has nothing to do with the topic and will leave your learner asking, "why?"

Now figure out if you are standing or sitting. If standing, don't rock back and forth on your feet too much (I'm talking to myself here). If you are sitting, don't sit in the squeakiest chair in North America (again, I'm guilty of this!). Remember, we're focusing on eliminating distractions or detractions from quality.

More items for consideration when eliminating distractions:

- Make eye contact with the camera.

- Wear timeless clothing.
- Don't flash your hands too much.
- Don't place your hands on the same surface as your microphone. You'll inevitably make unwanted noise.
- Use a good webcam and microphone (more on this soon). Poor quality audio is worse than poor quality video. Poor quality is a distraction.

Obviously, cameras are super important. Choosing a camera may seem intimidating or complex if you don't consider yourself a tech person. No worries, I'll make a few solid recommendations and you'll be recording in no time!

Ideally, you want a camera that can shoot at 4k or better resolution. For quality video, a minimum should be full high-definition at 1080p. If you've seen a video online or in a course and thought the image was grainy or fuzzy, chances are the person did not use a high-definition camera or needed more light.

Again, full high-definition at 4k is amazing. My favorite *4k webcam* for affordability, ease of use, and quality is the Logitech BRIO. You can pick one up on Amazon.com for under $200. It plugs into a USB port, requires very little technical knowledge, has some customization options, and is of outstanding quality.

When I started out, I used a Logitech 920. That model was a 1080p camera. I was on a video call one day with someone, and I noted the exceptional clarity of their picture. They were using the Logitech BRIO! I had heard so much about that camera. So, I decided to pick one up. It impressed me with how easy it was to set up and use. It's my go-to web camera.

I also love the video capture on my smartphone (a Samsung S21 Plus). Depending on when you're reading this book, that may or may not be hilarious to you as the phone market improves so rapidly. The quality of my Samsung S21 video recording is outstanding. Some people are super relieved when I recommend their smartphone as an option because they're very familiar with the functions.

Why make this complicated? If you can get a phone mount, pleasant light, and a top shelf smartphone, you can make some outstanding video.

If you want to step into the world of digital video cameras (not webcams), consider an affordable option like the Panasonic HC-V770. These, and similar full HD camcorders, won't break the bank and provide a significant upgrade over a webcam. This camera is my favorite for recording course videos!

I'll spare you a conversation on more advanced cameras. The options I've covered are all available under $1000. If you are interested in a better camera than those listed above, Google awaits!

Once you've assembled and set up your equipment, record a one-minute test video so you can see how quick and easy it is. It's important to not get in your head about it, so just do it! Done is better than perfect, and the sooner you start, the sooner you'll feel great about it.

Note: If videos and video production are a hurdle in your mind, there are simple solutions that I cover in my course, Monetize Your Book with a Course. Want a discount? Use discount code, BOOKNERD at checkout.

RECORDING AUDIO

The preferred method of presentation may be video, but audio *always* has the biggest impact on quality. Bad audio = bad course. No ifs, ands, or buts! Nothing turns a learner off faster than bad audio.

There are many simple factors to account for in recording quality audio for your lessons.

You can place mounted microphones on your desk or attach them to a stand or boom. Many of these microphones are now available with USB cables, so you can plug them directly into your computer without the need of a fancy interface device. Popular examples are the Blue Yeti and Rode NT-USB.

If you prefer to go with a wireless microphone, you can use a lapel-clipped lavalier microphone like the Samson Go Mic Mobile.

Just like lighting, the room you record in presents challenges for audio. You want a room that doesn't have a lot of hard flat surfaces creating a ton of echo. It's distracting when you log into someone's course, and there is an excessive hard surface echo in the recording. Record in a location that doesn't have this problem if you can. If it's possible to avoid speaking in the room corners, do so. The hard wall surfaces of corners increase the echo.

If you don't have options with the space, there are things you can do to reduce hard surface echo. You can cover your hard surfaces with soft fabrics. For desks, towels or T-shirts help. For larger surfaces like floors, throw carpets or blankets can reduce echo. You can install foam sound insulation on the walls if you really want to.

Microphone placement is important for reducing echo as well. Bring the microphone closer to your body, directly in front of you, and just out of view of the camera (above or below your head). This keeps you from having to project your voice while speaking. It also creates a more enjoyable experience as your student doesn't feel like they're being yelled at the whole time.

You also want to listen to the room before you record. Are there any sounds that you just didn't expect to be an issue? Like a piece of equipment running outside your window or someone cutting the grass or blowing leaves outside of your office? For me, it's the amazing package delivery guy (who I truly appreciate) showing up and making my dog go crazy. It's fun. These are the challenges of making video and audio recordings.

I have produced audio courses for my clients and my business. They are great, especially if there is a significant workbook component for the learner.

To summarize:

1. 1080p video is great, anything higher is fantastic. Reasonably priced webcam: Logitech Brio (under $200 USD). You can go up from there, but a great 1080p camera will get the job done with sufficient light. Speaking of light…
2. …Lighting makes all the difference in the world. Get some. Then get more.

3. Keep the videos to under 20 minutes each unless necessary (e.g., super complex topic requiring longer single lesson delivery).
4. The best part of video is great audio and a genuine delivery. Nail the audio quality in the video, learners will forgive some visual elements, but good audio is not negotiable. Neither is being real.
5. Have fun with it! Video is so great for drawing learners into your world.

Now that your tech is ready, let's dive into what's next: figuring out the best way to deliver your course content to your learner.

CHAPTER THREE:

MANAGING YOUR CONTENT

As an instructor, helping your learner get the most out of your content is key for several reasons. One, you want the learner to feel like they can learn the content. Two, you want them to feel like the content is manageable. And finally, you want them to feel successful when they've learned it.

To that end, the pace and amount of content you deliver is entirely up to you, just keep those three ideas in mind.

DRIP CONTENT

Drip content is a way to control the amount of content we expose a learner to in a set period. Simply put, you only release a certain amount of your course to the learner at a time.

You may release several lessons in the first week, the next series of lessons the following week, and a third series of lessons in the third week. You can carry this out if you'd like until the student finishes the course and completes the curriculum on the set schedule you created with your drip.

There is more than one way to structure early course launches!

ON-DEMAND, WITH LIVE CONTENT

Why would you want to do this? Let's look at the example of a coaching program. Perhaps you have a multi-week coaching program, which runs for eight weeks or two months. In those eight weeks, you want to focus your students on a set amount of curriculum each week. This keeps them from getting too far ahead of themselves or falling behind and gives them a specific target to aim for each week.

Each week, you give your clients access to live virtual group coaching sessions. You meet with those clients on the first day and tell them exactly how the program will run (course introduction). You explain that you'll meet with them weekly for live question-and-answer (Q&A) sessions as a group. Between the live Q&A sessions, you will provide them with a new drip of content or a new set of lessons to focus on for the week.

Finally, you'll wrap up that introduction meeting and release the first set of content to your program participants.

Now your clients only have access to that first set of lessons, and they will focus on that material throughout the week. That material may include informative videos, recorded instruction with audio and video, workbook sections, and maybe additional resources that you provide for them. Then, they will meet with you at the next week's Q&A session, and you will review the material from that week.

After reviewing the previous week's topic, you can then introduce them to the next week's topic and tell them exactly how you want them to approach the lessons. Then you release (drip) the next set of lessons to them.

You meet with them again the following week to cover the new material before introducing them to the next week's material. You repeat this flow until you deliver all the curriculum and live Q&As, at which point a live closing session is appropriate.

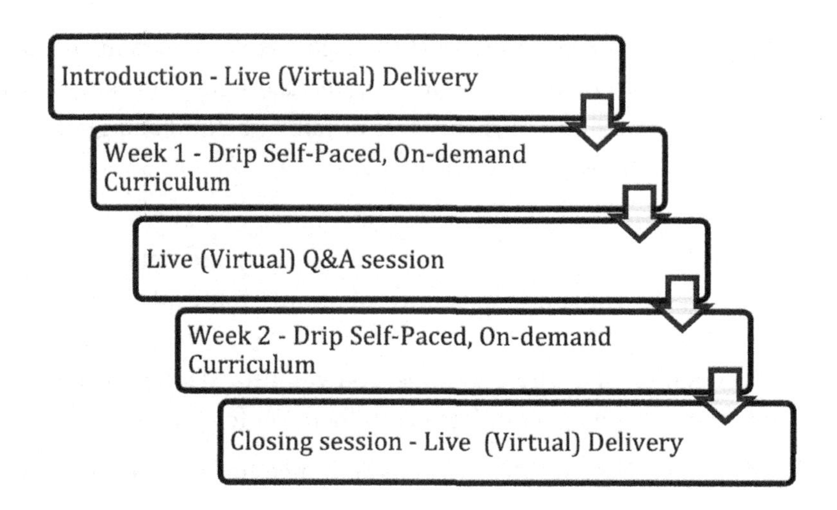

As you can see, the repetition creates a course rhythm and paces the learner. This is very effective for groups of learners in a cohort.

ON-DEMAND, NO LIVE CONTENT

What if you have a completely on-demand course with no live elements, and you want to pace the learner? No problem. Drip release to the rescue.

You can drip content to the learner every day, every week, or every two weeks, etc., and pick the release rate based on the material and the learner.

This drip content approach is ideal for a course being built in real time while learners attend the course! That's right, while you are developing the next release of material, your learners are fully engaged with the recent release.

In this self-paced course example, you may create new content while your students are engaged in your course. You build your course outline and show them the curriculum they are investing in on a course landing page.

You agree to release the content on a drip schedule that provides the students with material sooner rather than later. They agree that they'd rather access the material one release at a time, and off you go with a drip schedule. Now, you develop and upload the first chapter of the course.

The students start the self-paced course with the first chapter of material waiting for them in the learning management system. Then, as they work through the first chapter of information, you develop and publish the second chapter and release it on a set date.

Again, the cycle repeats; the students engage in the second chapter of dripped material while you create the third chapter. You continue to follow this format until you've developed and delivered all the curricula to your learners. Since this is a completely on-demand course, you don't have the live Q&A sessions.

LIVE BETA CONTENT ON A DRIP

There's one last way to consider drip content as a tool in your toolbox, and that is to create a course that your clients are absolutely clamoring to get their hands on, and it has a live component to it every week.

You can instruct the course live via a virtual application like Zoom or Teams (or whatever online platform you choose). Then you record each of those live teaching sessions with those students. You put them on a weekly schedule or a multi-day schedule. You meet with them for one to two hours and teach the material in those live sessions. After you record the live sessions, you load the recordings into the learning management system for student access later.

Clients love live instruction. But it helps to record because life gets in the way, or sometimes a student will have a significant commitment at the same time as the course. They don't want to miss out, so they sign up and attend as many of the live sessions as they can. Those who can't attend live simply review the recording later.

As an instructor, it's fantastic because this could be a beta for you. You may decide it's worth creating an on-demand course for future use. You can use a single live course to test that theory and deliver it live (virtually). Then, ask your clients how they feel about the post-session recordings, content, and pace, and whether the course met their expectations. You can do all of this with a live group of beta students or students in a beta course and refine your product for the next round.

Of course, if you're going to use the group of students as a beta, you may provide them with a financial discount knowing that it's not quite the finished product. Then, you'll ask them to take part in a preview on the drip schedule.

Afterward, you may decide that the course in its final, digestible form is better suited for self-paced, full access, and that's perfectly fine. Here, you may use a drip schedule to produce the course in its first iteration, or in a beta test, and then change the format to a fully accessible, fully self-paced course later. This is fine.

As you can see, drip content can be pretty sweet.

My advice is to use drip content where it makes sense and avoid it where it does not. As you have noticed in this book, I'm all about logic. Or at least I try to be.

It must make sense for the learner to benefit from the drip content. Never sacrifice the quality of the course or experience because you are in a rush to develop a course. However, if it doesn't negatively affect the learner to receive the content on a drip schedule, and it makes sense for you to produce it that way, well then, *rock and roll.*

In conclusion, drip content can provide you and your learners with some positive flexibility and is a way to control the pace of material in both a developmental and finished state.

MINICOURSES

Let's talk about how to package your course and the different forms or types of course packages that may benefit you and your learner.

As a business owner, you are moving a product. So, you expect a positive financial return on your investment. That means you need to move the *right* product.

Arguably, there isn't a factor more important than product packaging for moving products.

In an earlier analogy, we talked about the cover art and quality of a book. We also must determine whether we want a series of books or if we want a single book that's lengthy but complete.

When you wrote your book, you had the option of being a solo writer or including several writers in an anthology. With your course, the options are the same. Do you want to instruct alone, or have several instructors?

Do you want to sell your book as a print only, as an eBook, or more simply, in a downloadable PDF file?

These are different ways to package your book. You might even combine your book with another book. Say you produce your nonfiction book and couple it with a workbook that helps to guide your learner. I did this by publishing this book's companion workbook, *Monetize Your Book with a Course Guide: The Companion to Monetize Your Book with a Course.*

Are your readers able to see performance results by taking the steps outlined in your book?

When we look at packaging our courses, we will consider a few similar options.

Let's start with the most common, which is a complete course. It's one course that contains all the lessons on the topic you're teaching.

In the example of painting a cat, there would be just one course. Everything you are teaching people about painting cats is in that course. It lives in your learning management system as a single point of learning. Your student enrolls in your course, and they work from start to finish with a single product. (Note that I didn't say they'd start from "scratch.") I digress.

That is a typical single-course approach.

That course would have a landing page that introduces prospective students to all the wonderful things about your course. They could purchase the course, enroll in it, and have access to it.

I recommend that your online sales checkout process goes through a landing page.

Now, what if we have this big, wonderful course, and we suspect people will be interested in buying individual modules or chapters of that course at a smaller price? Maybe they don't need or want the whole thing. But they want a few of the key chapters, and those chapters have standalone value—meaning someone would realistically buy that chapter by itself.

Well, you may sell those chapters as minicourses.

You heard that right. But I wouldn't just take your big course, break it up, and not continue to offer that course. From the business perspective, this doesn't mean making a choice between offering a complete course *or* a minicourse. The idea is to offer both complete courses *and* minicourses.

So, take your complete course and publish it.

Then take that course and replicate the select sections to create smaller course packages.

Keep the complete course content structure as close to original as possible, meaning whatever you move, keep it intact. So, if you create a minicourse out of a chapter, replicate the original chapter structure as much as possible.

Remember, everything's based on logic here; if it makes sense to do it, then do it. But if it doesn't make sense to do it, don't!

If you decide to move forward with a minicourse, you need to create an introduction to that new product. Determine whether the introduction video to your complete course is sufficient for this purpose. Nine times out of ten, it will not be. Unless that original introduction is generic, you'll want to create a specific introduction video. This could be anywhere from thirty seconds to three minutes long, so it's not a big lift to record a new one.

Build your new minicourse just like you built the complete course. Set up a landing page with checkout and enrollment options. If the course requires, or offers, a certificate upon completion, load and assign a certificate to the course.

Also, when you sell minicourses, you have a prime opportunity to upsell other minicourses from the same complete course. So, let's say you made two, or three, or six courses from the original whole course. You can congratulate people for completing the How to Paint Your Cat course and upsell them to the next minicourse. Right? You could say something as simple as, "I encourage you to attend the next course in the series: How to Tame an Angry Cat 101."

You may even consider providing your students with a discount on that next course to reward them for buying while they're satisfied with your product.

You don't have to offer a discount, but you have the opportunity, and it may be effective if that discount doesn't openly exist in other places. That motivates them to get the deal while the getting's good.

So, you've created a minicourse from a segment of your complete course. Now, you may wonder how to price it well, and several options are available to you.

My general rule of thumb is that if I broke a complete course into a bunch of minicourses, and in aggregate, those minicourses contain the total content of the complete course, I have created two different packages, and won't price them the same. Now, you may wonder how to price it well, and several options are available to you. I cover these options and more in my book, *Course Pricing Strategies.*

Price minicourses so that if someone purchases each of them, the total cost would be more than the cost of purchasing the complete course. Motivate your learner to buy the complete course and pay you the money in one shot. That added cost also allows you to be compensated for the work of breaking up your big course into a bunch of mini products. Yes, there is a lot of work involved, so you shouldn't feel bad about a little compensation.

For example, let's say you want to sell ten minicourses at $100 each, and your complete course contains ten chapters and sells for $1,000. That's perfectly fine. But do not go below $100.

If $100 is the floor, consider tacking on a fee of about 20% to each of those minicourse prices. That will make it more worthwhile to sell those minicourses.

That means we originally had a course with a cost of $1,000 to our students. We broke that up into ten minicourses, and if we priced those $100 for each, we wouldn't lose money. If we added 20% to those minicourses, each course would sell for $120. Then you'd have ten minicourses priced each at $120. If a student completed all your minicourses, they would pay $1,200.

There are obvious reasons for making that added 20%. Right? You're giving your students the benefit of not having to spend $1,000 in one shot. But you're selling them that benefit at $20, and that's a fair shake.

You had to start by setting up a whole new landing page. Beyond that, you manage multiple course sales instead of one product. So now you're managing eleven products, one complete course, and ten minicourses. That 20% is not much in the long run, considering the work required to build out and manage those minicourses. At the end of this lesson, we'll discuss the fact that you will have work that you didn't have before.

If someone were to take advantage of the added benefit and take all your classes for the additional cost of $20 each, they would spend $1200. But most people will not take all the classes, so let's understand that right now.

People who choose to take the minicourses rather than the complete course are most likely not going to buy all ten of your minicourses. If they do, congratulations, that's awesome.

You now have the opportunity we spoke about earlier; to upsell other minicourses by offering student incentives. You have that flexibility in your pricing because you set the price for every minicourse with a 20% bump up. Now there is 20% worth of wiggle room for upselling and offering discounts on future minicourses.

Let's look at an example:

We had one complete course that we broke up into ten minicourses. We priced each minicourse at a $100 base fee, plus 20%, equaling $120 for each minicourse.

Now a student completes their first minicourse. They love it and want to attend the next course. The final course slide offers them a discount code on the next course in the minicourse series, and it says something like, "I'm grateful that you enjoyed the first minicourse. If you feel like this was a great experience for you, I encourage you to enroll in the next course in the series. And if you do, I'll offer you a discount for being such a loyal, dedicated, and successful student."

Then, you offer them anywhere from 10 to 20% off the next minicourse. So, you're giving them an opportunity and motivating them to enroll in the next course and save 10 or 20%. That 10 or 20% is eating out of that additional fee that you put on top of the course, to begin with. So, you're not priced below your original base price.

Why is this important? Well, if I sell the complete course for $1,000, and I now sell ten minicourses for $100, I can't afford to give minicourse discounts without losing profit at the original course price. Word will get out quickly that you're offering discounts on the minicourses, but not on the complete course.

People will buy your minicourses to take advantage of the discounts, and you'll end up losing up to $200 worth of profit for each learner!

That is fine for some people and not for others. Different people have different perspectives on their money.

Just be intentional about your strategy. You can determine whether you see that as a risk to your business or not. Some people will say, "I'm not worried about that. I'm just glad they're motivated to buy courses, and I'm helping people, and if that's what sells courses, then great. I can always increase the price of the total course package to compensate other people."

They may try to keep the price as low as possible but barely pull the profit margin. Maybe they don't have much wiggle room but feel that their price is very fair. So, they're going to be a little more risk averse.

You can see a lot goes into making even small decisions, like breaking a flagship course into minicourses.

Earlier I made a point about configuration control. This creates additional work for you. When you create a single complete course, you manage the configuration, structure, information, and content of that single course.

When you decide to break it up into many courses, you now have additional courses to manage. Let's say you change a chapter in the big course. You update some of the information because the industry has changed, there's some new method, or you find new information that could be of value to your learners.

Instead of having to change just the complete course, you now must change the minicourses too. That means you double your change management workload by replicating or spinning off chapters into minicourses. You manage the configuration of two products but only benefit from the sale of one product.

Again, not a big deal if it's worth the money–I know plenty of people who will tell you it is because they have students who buy minicourses regularly.

Others rarely sell minicourses. Their students want the entire package, and they buy the complete course.

One of my last points on minicourses is that you'll need new course cards. You'll also need website copy and a pricing strategy.

If you print or distribute content about a portfolio of courses, you'll have to keep that up to date. Your academy webpage for your education offers will also have to include an updated listing of your courses.

Ultimately, there's a lot of additional copy and work involved in spinning off multiple courses.

So why do all this? Well, it can be very profitable.

I heard a story that illustrates this perfectly. There was an artist who taught people how to paint, and her clients normally met with her at the community center to take her painting classes. They were used to coming in for quick sessions and paying a cheap price.

So, she created a bunch of minicourses, each focused on a single topic of painting, and she sold them for $15. Over one year, she generated over $100,000 in core sales.

You read that right! $100,000 in revenue, selling $15 courses.

Now, she had a very healthy following that was so dedicated to her they quickly spread the word to their friends, who showed up and bought her minicourses, too.

Much like the success of an entire course depends upon marketing and sales, so does the success of a minicourse.

In closing, I highly encourage you to spin your whole course off into minicourses if it's something that you feel is manageable and profitable for your business.

Ask yourself some important "why" questions. Are you doing it because it's making a certain amount of money? Is it because you are helping clients you couldn't reach with the complete course? Is it because you offer a better solution to people across multiple income levels? What is it when you wake up that motivates you to have these additional products in your product line?

In the end, make product line decisions based on whether you'll be happy about that decision in the morning when you wake up. If you wake up tomorrow, are you going to be happy that you spun these off into minicourses?

Focus on your motivator. If you can make sense of the decision based on that motivation, and you know you would reap that benefit...

Then I say go for it.

COURSE BUNDLES

Course bundles are an excellent way to offer multiple courses to your learners in one package. This is often very helpful for students who are interested in several related courses.

It also gives you the opportunity to sell bundles of related courses at a discount. This works extremely well when you have a portfolio or category of related courses. For example, you may have one master class that comprises all lessons in one big course. And that's great. It's the flagship course for your business, and soon after launching, you realize you may benefit from having broken that course up into several shorter courses and offering them at lower prices to make your products more accessible and deliverable in bite sized packages. These are the minicourses we talked about earlier.

Let's say you have several minicourses, or a bunch of flagship courses, and you want to offer the group of those flagship courses or minicourses to your learners. You can do that with a bundle. They pay once and they're enrolled in all those courses in the bundle.

Pretty sweet for the learner because they only buy once and get access to multiple courses. It's sweet for you because you sell multiple courses in one checkout.

This is a very attractive option for people who are interested in several courses on a specific topic or genre. Kind of like buying a series of books!

You can also get creative and bundle a course with other products like live Q&A sessions, e-books, summits, a coaching program, or a symposium or conference.

Normally, the bundle price is equal to the cost of all included courses or a little less. I'm a big fan of the discounted approach because it motivates the learner to take advantage of this great deal and buy multiple courses with one press of a button. They save money and gain access to all the courses of interest to them.

Doesn't that sound great? It's good for them, and it's good for you. I'm a big fan of a win-win scenario.

When pricing the bundle, the discount amount is up to you. There's no golden rule. Just like when we discussed pricing your course, you want to discount enough for the learner to recognize the value of the deal easily without giving away too much. A discount in the 10%-30% range is normally a safe number.

GROUPING STUDENTS - GROUPS, COHORTS, AND COMMUNITIES

Let's talk about ways to organize your students while they're in your course. Once you've enrolled multiple learners in a course, you can decide whether you want to organize them in groups based on a few factors. Two major benefits of grouping students include administrative functions and interactivity. This will be much clearer in a moment, I promise!

Groups organize students within the learning management system. You can use groups to track the progress of multiple learners for a single organization. For example, you may have sold ten seats in your course to a business client, and the manager asks about weekly progress reports for their people. The employee's identity as a member of the business's account makes their experience unique.

That's one example of how grouping them may be a good idea.

Let's explore an example of a non-interactive student group scenario. You build and launch a course in your learning management system, and ten students enroll and start your course a week later.

Outstanding. Everything's off to a great start.

The course is self-paced, with a group coaching session once a week. Your students log into the learning management system and complete the on-demand material at their convenience. They are not interacting with other students or the instructor in real time. You have ten students enrolled in the course, and you want to send them emails or special materials, or track student performance metrics (e.g., completion percentages, logins).

Perhaps you want to organize students in cohorts, a group that goes through the course together in a certain period, and you want them grouped to document that. In the future, well after that group of students has passed through the course, you will know which version of your course they attended and when.

You can also group students depending on your desire for them to interact. For example, you may have a group of learners in a course with accountability buddies, group collaboration sessions, and group projects. It is nice to email each group, when necessary, assess group performance, and provide them with a means of being easily identified in the learning management system (LMS).

Now let's take group benefits one step further. Let's say you have a cohort of students attending your self-paced course. They are remote and have no connection or affiliation with each other outside of your course. They know other students are in the course and are free to interact. However, there is no way for them to communicate outside of email. If you want to fix that and give them better options, consider launching discussion boards or a community!

Digital communities are a value proposition for learners. You can group students from one or more courses into communities. For example, in the Thinkific learning management system, you can create a community for learners, instructors, general fans, or whoever you feel is appropriate as a community member! You can give them community access based on their interest in a particular topic or course that you offer.

Communities provide a truly interactive experience in an on-demand course. This is a tremendous advantage over other on-demand courses that require the student to work alone.

Would you prefer to be a part of a course consumed in isolation or one with the opportunity to engage with others? (Hint: only one of these gives you options.)

The first level of interaction in the curriculum is an on-lesson discussion. These discussions allow students to comment on topics when the moment is right in a lesson.

Let's look at on-lesson discussions in action. Your student attends a course lesson or completes one of your workbook lessons, and they have comments or questions about the topic. They can jump into an on-lesson discussion to ask a question or leave a comment that the instructor and other students can see. As the instructor, you'll receive an email notification that Student A submitted a comment to the discussion board. You can log into the discussion board to respond to their comments and questions and perhaps use the opportunity to expand on the lesson content. Within a few minutes, a few other students see the comments in their notifications and join the conversation.

You can view the on-lesson discussion and interact with the students via text or uploads (e.g., images, documents, links).

A community expands on this concept. It gives your students a digital meeting space for engagement and connection with other students. This digital community is home to living discussion boards focused on specific topics, live events (e.g., workshops, live Q&A sessions, group coaching sessions, meet and greet events, and live instruction), and file exchanges.

Do you currently host *live* events, one-on-one coaching, or learning sessions in your courses? Perhaps you provide in-person events for people in a specific area or region. Naturally, these events present geographic or time limitations for online students. They aren't just sitting in an open virtual meeting all day, waiting for people to enter and leave at will. Digital communities provide the opportunity to post timely updates, grow a following, and host events.

Communities have the added benefit of taking students out of the course environment where the curriculum is king and bringing them into a community where they can collaborate or interact and in which you can add value to keep them engaged. That interaction provides students with a rich and immersive experience while you grow and nurture your following of loyal fans. Communities have expanded over the years in learning and learning management systems because of the popularity of communities on social platforms like Facebook, LinkedIn, Slack, and Circle.

Traditionally, you had to maintain two different sites: a learning management system and some social media site to put these functions together. However, LMS providers have seen the value of these communities and wisely launched communities. This is a substantial offer for course hosts because our students don't have to leave the LMS to take part in a community. We want to keep them engaged in the course environment and *away* from the distractions of social media sites. You want to capture your student's attention, not compete with Aunt Linda's cat photos and your 2nd cousin's political rants (aren't those just *the best?*). Even better, you don't have to manage multiple platforms and the cost and administrative burden of both.

Communities add tremendous value to your course. Sometimes, they can be the single most valuable element of your course because of the volume of learning, interaction, and relationships built in the community. When you consider the value of that experience over time, it really adds up.

The goal is to build a healthy, interactive, informative community experience for your learners.

Once you've built this awesomeness, consider how long you will provide access to the community. You may choose to keep the community live for the same dates that the course is live. In this example, students would enroll in your course, complete your curriculum, and have access to the community while enrolled. When the course expires, or the student drops from the course, their community access expires. In this model, you combine access to the course and community. This is a restrictive model, not necessarily one that I advise, but some people find it useful.

The next model is a community that continuously runs despite the length or future state of the course. So, let's say you enroll students in a 90-day course. They complete the course and keep access to the active community. (Great job, moderator!) You keep the community alive and thriving by regularly interacting, encouraging member participation, and consistently providing valuable content. The course experience is complete, and the members are taking full advantage of the community element of your learning experience.

Another option is to make the course and community indefinitely available to your students. You don't have to worry about course expiration dates. Your job is to keep people engaged and provide your members with a positive and professional experience for as long as the community exists. You fill it with course attendees and focus on engagement.

Now, sometimes, you may choose not to have a course but still to have a community. You may ask, "Look, why are you telling me about this? This entire book is about creating courses. Are you telling me I don't have to own a course?" Yes, I am.

You may decide to do everything within a community and make the community the learning experience for the students, and you may decide to add content and value to the community via a resource library. This means you enroll learners in this community for a free or paid membership and provide them access to a resource library containing files, video, audio, and text and PDF files. You could also provide other resources, like web links or external sites, that you feel are valuable to your community members. And you can either market and sell to your community or just use it as a gathering place for free. It's up to you.

The free resource library approach, rather than a course, is very helpful. If you don't want to be pressured into structuring the course before you develop your community, you can develop the community around the premise that you have a course in development. You're also providing community members with access to resources now rather than later and offering that for a low monthly subscription. An additional benefit is that they also receive a new community of people to meet and communicate with.

I recommend you have a few base elements in your community. First, you should have a space within that community for new members to introduce themselves. After they log in, you would ask them to enter information about themselves for other members of the community to see. Essentially, this is an opportunity for them to walk into the virtual room, say hello, and introduce themselves. They will tell people who they are, where they live, what they do for a living, why they're in the community, what they hope to get out of their experience in the community, and what they hope to provide others while they're in the community. That post can stand in the system indefinitely.

People will always know that they can go to the introduction space and find out more about somebody. As a moderator of a community, I ask every new member to introduce themselves. It's nice to kick that introduction off with a post to welcome them, which prompts the other members to welcome them too.

You could post, for example: Please welcome our newest member, Lucas Marino, to *The Cat Painters Posse.*

My second recommendation is to post your community guidelines. These communicate your expectations, and direct community members on what's acceptable and what is not in their behavior and interactions.

Many communities offer the ability to have spaces dedicated to specific topics. In that community, you can host live events, create spaces around unique topics or product experiences, and you can even host giveaways. You can also share exclusive offers and sales that you don't share with members of any other community, or with the public.

These are nice ways to reward your members for being active in your community. It also keeps them engaged and gives them something to check on. No one wants to miss out on a good sale. But much like your course, it's up to you to keep people engaged and to create an environment and community where people want to interact. Make sure they feel safe and have an enjoyable experience.

INSTRUCTOR PROFILE AND BIO

As a course instructor, people will be interested in learning more about who you are. Your students will normally want to see an instructor bio in two places: on your course landing page, and in the course.

Be careful with the instructor's bio. Short and sweet is nice, but like everything else in your course, it has a purpose. You should not use your bio as an opportunity to brag about how great you are or all the great things you've accomplished. The purpose is to give the learner confidence that you're the right instructor for them and that you have the requisite experience and credentials.

Provide relevant information only. Save the long story about how you got where you are and where you came from for the *About Me* page of your website.

Go ahead and list any relevant credentials or education degrees. Talk about what you do for a living, what your passion is, why you've launched this course, and what you want for your student. Be short and sweet–one paragraph and, of course, a fancy headshot.

In the Thinkific LMS example, this all gets loaded in an instructor bio card or an instructor bio link. You can load your bio in the LMS, and it will automatically populate in areas of the site when you select an instructor bio as a part of a page. It's cool; you can load it once and use it all over your website. You can use it on landing pages, in the course, and on pages for free resources. Essentially, you've got an entire website at your disposal; you can put it anywhere you think it would be helpful.

Now let's talk about that headshot you've been using. It wouldn't have made sense to post a picture of your company's logo or a picture of anything other than you. This is especially important in an online course. In most instances, the student is never actually going to meet you. They're going to attend this class online without ever actually seeing you face to face. Also, if you're asking for a significant investment from your learner in tuition for enrollment fees, they most likely won't buy if they don't see the face of the instructor. Do yourself a favor and get a pleasant picture. If you don't know which picture to use, consider using the same headshot you would use for your LinkedIn profile.

If you don't want to use something too professional and you're trying to show a relaxed image, it still needs to be professional. Pictures of you drinking and going to a football game may not be the best choice. Unless, of course, you're teaching a course about how to drink beer at a football game. In that case, it's 100% relevant.

You get the point. I'm very tempted to post a picture of me holding a cat covered in paint. I digress.

COMPLETION CERTIFICATES

Let's talk about course certificates. Sometimes they are required, and sometimes they are not.

When students need to prove that they completed a course by a certain date on a specific topic, with a particular education provider, a course certificate will be required. Normally, there are a few key entries on a completion certificate, including the course title, date of completion, training provider (your company), the name of the student, and the hours of course attendance.

You may have a course that meets professional development unit requirements for a professional certification, qualification, or licensure program. The organizations that control those certifications and licenses require that the student complete a set number of hours of training a year. The topic, the training period, and the provider may be required to be pre-screened and approved by those organizations. For example, I'm a member of the Project Management Institute, which is an organization that has pre-certified education providers and learning resources for professional development units, or credits toward recertification.

As a Project Management Professional, I can attend a course and present my certificate of completion to the Project Management Institute. They will then grant me the pre-approved number of credits. That's pretty sweet, right?

This space is also very lucrative for companies. If you weren't listening before, I hope you're listening now. I have seen several companies produce courses that are required by local, state, or federal governments, and those courses are in high demand because of that formal requirement. The same applies to professional certification and licensing bodies. If you produce courses for any of these, make sure that you meet the certification requirements of those bodies. You also need to make your course available to the people in their population who require those credits or units.

As you can see, certificates carry a lot of significance in that situation. But even when a certificate is not required, it's just nice to have one proving you did something professional.

It's a badge of honor, and in many cultures, it's expected to earn a certificate of completion. If you sell courses globally, expect an increased interest in completion certificates.

CHAPTER FOUR:

COURSE CRITIQUES, REVIEWS, AND TESTIMONIALS

Okay, so once you've wrapped up delivery of all your actionable or informative course material, and it's time to wrap your course up, there are still a few things you're going to want to do.

Before you shut off the lights and lock the doors, remember the old saying: *Tell them what you're going to tell them. Tell them. Then tell them what you told them.*

Well, we're going to do a little of that at the end of each chapter, or at a minimum, at the end of the course. You'll want to review the course objectives, and goals.

If your course helped students close any performance gaps, it's a good time to briefly outline those gaps at a high level. Many of you did this in your book's conclusion or closing chapters.

We want to bring the learner's focus back to the primary goals and objectives for several reasons. One of which is to make sure they didn't miss something. Another is to help them identify if there are any weak points remaining at the end of the course that they should go back and review. Maybe there is some material that they didn't quite grasp fully, and they may need a second pass.

CHAPTER AND COURSE SURVEYS

Another thing we're going to want to do is an end-of-chapter, or an end-of-course survey.

We sometimes refer to these as reviews. But I'm going to avoid using the word review in this application because we're going to use that as a separate thing, and I want to avoid confusion. So, let's use the words survey or critique.

An end-of-chapter or end-of-course survey or critique is an opportunity for you to ask questions and allow your learner to ask questions and get feedback on how well the course met their needs. I'm talking about all their needs.

Did the course help them reach their goals? Did the objectives of the course help the learner close the performance gap? Was the material presented properly and appropriately?

The point of gathering this feedback is to improve the course for future learners, and to determine customer satisfaction. You may recall that courses have creative, technical, and administrative elements. We want to touch on each of those elements. We also want to determine whether the learner thought that this experience was worth their while. We may completely satisfy them with the content and quality of the course. But they may not feel like it was necessary. There's nothing wrong with it. They just wouldn't do it twice, or recommend it to a friend, because it wasn't necessary.

We need to know those things. We also need to know if there was anything that we didn't cover that the student wished we had. What was good or bad about the course?

Here are some sample questions that you can consider for your course:

- Was the online format helpful, hurtful, or neutral?
- Did the live Q&A sessions help you?
- Were the animations and interactive content helpful?
- Did you like the interactive digital workbook, or would you prefer the downloadable PDF?

- Please rate your level of satisfaction with the length of the course.
- Please rate your level of satisfaction with the quality of the recorded materials.
- Please rate your level of satisfaction with the instructor's presentation style.
- Did the LMS present any technical challenges?
- Would you recommend this course to your friends and family?
- Would you recommend this course to your co-workers?
- What course would you like to see next?
- Was there any material that wasn't covered that you hoped would be covered?
- Rate your level of satisfaction with the length of the lessons and chapters.
- Did you experience difficulties accessing your course in the LMS?
- Is there anything you'd like to share with the instructor?

As you can see, there's a lot we can ask people on the way out of the course. You wouldn't want to ask all these questions at the conclusion of a chapter. Keep chapter summaries brief. People want to move on to the next lesson. Limit end-of-chapter surveys to 3-5 questions, then move to the next chapter.

Also, be careful how often you use end-of-chapter surveys. No one wants to complete 20 surveys in a single course.

This is one reason I hold my survey at the end of the course. However, if I had a multi-week course, I may do a survey once a week. This way I can adjust the following week's curriculum if needed. Otherwise, a single end-of-course review or critique is probably all you'll need.

STUDENT REVIEWS

Student reviews are more like testimonials, and your learning management system may have a student review capture built into it. It will just be something generic that asks the learner to share their thoughts on the course and will have an open text field so they can freely type their opinion. The reason many of your learning management systems provide this separate student review function is that it makes it easy to use those comments in your social proofs on your landing page.

Remember, student reviews and testimonials, when used as a social proof, provide potential learners with the opinion of former students. It helps them see that other people have taken this class and have enjoyed it; found it useful and valuable. That's great.

Capturing a student review in the learning management system makes it very easy to load those reviews to your landing and home pages. You wouldn't normally use comments from the end-of-course reviews as a social proof, but if you want that option, say that in the review or critique form. You ask the student's permission to use their comment for those purposes.

Chapter and course reviews are an intimate and powerful way for you to determine the satisfaction of your learners with your course. Student reviews and testimonials are a powerful way to share the good news and opinions about your course with potential learners.

EDITING AND BETA TESTING

Once your course is complete, you will be in a similar situation to when you finished writing your book. You've created the course card, which is like the cover of your book. You've created the landing page, which is like the back cover of your book.

You've filled your course with all the great information and fun activities to reinforce what you've taught your learner. Now you need a quality review of your product, much like your book needed an editor.

I'm blessed with an amazing editor, Karen Hunsanger. Karen edited this book in lockstep with me every day as I wrote. You most likely will not take this same approach with your course. You might not require an editor to crawl over your pages of awesomeness. However, you'll reach a point when you need someone to review your material.

There are a few options here. You can hire an independent course developer or editor to go through your course as a learner and provide critical feedback. You can also create a small beta group and ask them to attend your course and provide that critical feedback so you can make revisions before the release to the public. You may choose both options!

Assembling your beta group is much like choosing an advanced reader group for your book. The pilot group shouldn't be made of family members, best friends, and people who are in your closest circle. The members need to fit the profile of your ideal learner—the person you designed this course around.

Your beta group needs to reflect your ideal learner so that you can inject as much of their perspective into the course as possible.

Once your beta group has attended your course and provided you with course feedback, you're going to capitalize on their attendance by requesting a testimonial. This beta group's testimonial is going to be critical to future marketing efforts because you can post their testimonials on your course landing page, or on your home website as evidence of how great your program is for your ideal learner. Don't miss this opportunity to gather testimonials, much like when you were looking for those early readers' five-star reviews for your Amazon profile.

Your beta group is also serving as a quasi-editor. You should provide them the opportunity to give feedback on every aspect of the course. Did the lessons flow in a logical order? Was the content in the appropriate format? Meaning, did the quizzes help? Did the interactive nature of the course live up to their expectations? Was the course entertaining enough?

Yes, people need to be entertained in training.

The more you can entertain and educate them simultaneously, the better their experience will be. Was the platform intuitive and helpful? Did they have any problems with the download files? Were the links to external sites and resources functional and helpful?

These are some questions we're going to ask most of our future students when we are digging into some gears in the course's machine.

If you don't want to ask the future learners all these questions, ask them some basics.

What did you think of the course thumbnail image?

What did you think of the landing page?

Who do you know that could benefit from this course?

This is one way of lead capture.

It's also a way of discovering new learner types for your course. You may have designed your course for one specific group of people, not even realizing it could benefit a whole other group. And one of your beta students sees it clear as day, recommends this learner type to you, and you include the new group in your marketing strategy.

Ask them even more detailed questions. Was there anything distracting on the landing page? Anything too cheesy or salesy? What did you think of the color scheme? Essentially, you're asking them to do a site and course assessment.

You need to make this as easy for them as possible. I prefer to use a survey form inside the course player. Build it right into the course as one of the last lessons. Use this special survey for your beta group, and after the beta is done, determine whether to remove it and inject your previously designed survey for regular learners.

Lastly, you want to ask them: What do you need next? What do you want next? This group may have some fantastic ideas for follow-on courses. Take advantage of that experience. Then, after you've collected all their feedback, consider how much more of that feedback you want from your next round of course attendees.

How much additional feedback do I want to gather from my learners now that the beta is done? You can merge the survey that you developed for your regular learners and the survey that you developed for your beta learners into one updated survey for your regular course attendees.

You have creative freedom here. Just be careful not to overload them. No one wants that. If they're a part of your beta group, they should expect to provide extensive feedback, but regular students should not. The expectations are different.

Whereas the beta group normally attends for free or at a significantly discounted price, for that expected level and depth of detailed feedback.

Now that you've received feedback about your course, your landing page, and about the learner's experience with your curriculum, it's time to implement changes. When reviewing the feedback from your beta testers and students, some of the obvious changes will jump out of the survey. There may be a unanimous consent that an aspect of the course was fantastic, and there may be a consensus that certain elements were not as fantastic.

Wherever you see a consensus, the default answer should be to incorporate that feedback into your course. For items only brought up by one or a few beta students, take a moment to consider if it will improve the material and the learner's experience, then come back to it later, after the first round.

Since we're making changes based on feedback, you're going to have to bear with me for a moment. As a systems engineer, I highly recommend you keep a change log of all the changes you make. It's just in my DNA.

If you have a very large course, or a very comprehensive course, it's not a bad idea to keep a change log. This way, you know when you enacted a change and how it affected your course. You also want to list the justification for the change. Those would be the bare minimum.

Over time, you may find that keeping a change log is unnecessary, and you can discontinue it. But it sure is nice to have at your disposal when you need it in the future. You may even decide to publish that change log in some form for your learners in evergreen courses, because they may be interested in seeing how the course has changed over the years.

What if you provided lifetime access to one of your courses on a very complex topic, and something changes with regulations, laws, or certifications? If I previously attended your course, I would come back to that course material. If you've kept the course updated, it would be helpful to see the change log so that I know the changes made in the course since I last attended. Then I can decide to update my skills or knowledge by completing those lessons.

In conclusion, it's helpful to have a group of professional people review your product and provide you with feedback before you release it to the public. It's not required, but it is useful, and the feedback can help you improve your product before you put it out into the world. Of course, like all things, you need to use your judgment to determine whether you have the time and if it's necessary. As you become more experienced with course development, you may decide to bypass the beta group altogether. However, as I've become more experienced, I've become more dependent on beta groups. I don't want to spend the time marketing and promoting a course that isn't going anywhere or won't help people.

You can have a great idea, and it's not the right thing; it's just not going to have legs. It doesn't make it less important or valuable. It just changes the way you prioritize the development and promotion of that product. For now, spend your energy doing something else.

You are running a business. You have priorities. You need to consider this as part of your business strategy.

We've covered a lot in this chapter, but we're really just getting warmed up. You'll want to know how to choose a learning management system that will be a true asset to your course and your business. When you're ready to take a deeper dive in your learning management system, turn the page!

CHAPTER FIVE:

COURSE CREATOR TECHNOLOGY

If I had to pick one topic as the most intimidating to course creators, I would pick technology. There is a seemingly endless sea of tech waiting for course creators and the anxiety of picking and learning new technology can cause real damage to your confidence and motivation.

Fear not, friends. I'm going to simplify things and get you on the path to delivering courses like a pro. To do so, let's get more familiar with that wonderful tool I mentioned in the previous chapter–a learning management system.

WHAT THE HECK IS A LEARNING MANAGEMENT SYSTEM?

A learning management system (LMS) is software that helps you assemble, publish, and deliver your course to your learners. Think about the LMS as the website where your course lives.

Some commercially available LMSs include Thinkific (my favorite), Kajabi, Teachable, Canvas, Blackboard, Matrix, and many more. It seems like each day, some snazzy new LMS hits the market, claiming to be everything for everyone.

In reality, each LMS company focuses its efforts on a particular type of product functionality and quality. Some LMSs, like Thinkific, strive to be a higher-quality option and present a professional, intuitive platform. They intentionally avoid becoming a hybrid LMS-CRM-Marketing machine that does most things decently, but nothing very well. They focus on making the creation and publication of courses easy and the presentation of those courses to students, professional and intuitive. You can build your courses, course landing pages, and website on a platform like Thinkific and know that you will have a professional product.

Some LMSs try to be everything for everyone. This is a noble aspiration, but it's very hard to achieve. They degrade the quality of the LMS to prop up other desirable functions normally associated with Customer Relationship Management (CRM) software. The LMS gets watered down as a tradeoff for other features like contact management, email hosting, and e-commerce features.

Then there are the cheaper options. These lower-tier LMSs provide a minimum level of functionality. They make their money catering to a low-budget creator who doesn't want to spend much on quality and is merely publishing a course for the lowest possible price. This is the Udemy crowd.

Choosing a platform with shallow features may cause your courses and site to fall short of quality in areas of significance.

Naturally, the lowest-quality, lowest-price approach presents quality risks to serious entrepreneurs. If your LMS is of inferior quality, you cannot, in good conscience, publish a high-value, high-dollar course on the platform. Your clients will be unwilling to pay hundreds or thousands of dollars when the quality is inferior. It's like trying to sell a brand-new Mercedes-Benz at a low-budget car dealership in a shady part of town. Chances are, the right buyer isn't shopping in your area, and if they are, they will most likely prefer to spend their $160,000 at a nicer dealership.

If you are in the market for a professional course from a consultant, author, coach, or other creative with a strong reputation for quality, you expect that person to publish a quality course on a quality platform.

Let's consider a familiar example: *a book.*

When you get your hands on a printed book, you can *immediately* determine its quality. The binding is strong. The cover art and title are clear and enticing. The cover material isn't rough, flimsy, or creased.

The publisher appropriately spaced the print on the pages in an appealing font and size. Uniform margins prevail throughout the book.

The back cover copy is void of spelling and grammatical errors, and draws you to the premise of the book, and its fantastic testimonials build your confidence that this is a must-read!

You can *feel* it when you have a well-published book in your hand. It's a very tactile experience. It's an appealing product. You're willing to spend your hard-earned money on a quality publication.

What would you think if you picked up that same book containing all the same words but printed on much cheaper, thin pages? Maybe the typeset has a little bleed or runoff. The binding feels flimsy, so you know the pages aren't going to stay in place for very long. These things deter you from wanting to spend more money on the product.

Suddenly, that $50 book isn't worth it. It's the same way with your courses. If you don't spend the time to develop a quality course and publish it on a quality LMS, then you're taking away from the value of your learner's experience and producing an inferior product.

Now, I'm not saying that everyone should spend a fortune on the most expensive software because expensive software is thought to indicate better quality. I'm not saying that at all. You need to experiment a bit to find the best fit for you.

However, there are some acknowledged standards in the industry right now, and it would be silly of us to ignore them.

If you're interested in acquiring a free Thinkific account, check out this link: https://try.thinkific.com/s11dibi7sb58

Full disclosure: *I'm a certified Thinkific expert, and an affiliate. I will always recommend Thinkific as my preferred platform because it's what I use; it delivers the quality I expect for my clients.*

Now, what does an LMS do?

Well, you can host products in an LMS, like courses, virtual summits, and enrollment webinars. All the things that you can sell digitally, you can sell or list in a learning management system.

You can deliver viewable or downloadable PDF documents, animated videos, text files, text content on screen, and audio files, which could be recordings of podcasts or other audio files from your videos. You can put any digital product in a learning management system.

Each learner, instructor, or administrator has their own account. In their account, they have access to all the courses they're enrolled in.

People with different roles have different capabilities within the system. A learner can view course pages, course content, and published website pages. An instructor can load and interact with content in a designated course. An administrator can make site changes, which may include pricing, funds collection, tracking student progress, affiliate performance, and the changing settings or content on web pages, landing pages, and home pages.

As you can see, a lot goes into a learning management system. You may consider a learning management system that can do everything you want it to do, including serving as your main website. This is what I do with my Thinkific sites. I use my Thinkific sites as my primary website and my course delivery product or platform.

Essentially, the LMS is the carrier of your message. The LMS presents your material to the learner. It's where they go to interact with your content, your brand, and your message. Therefore, choosing the right LMS is critically important.

Does your LMS allow learners to complete digital workbook files, interact in private communities, and consume all recorded material in the same course player? These elements of interaction improve the learner's experience and reflect positively on your brand.

CONTENT CREATION TECHNOLOGY AND TOOLS

One thing that intimidates many first-time course creators is the technology involved in building, hosting, and managing courses. Many of my clients tell me they tried to start on their own but quickly became overwhelmed by the large number of technical tools and applications targeting course creators.

There's a perception that it takes a bucket load of different tools to do everything needed to build, launch, and sustain a course. Just as in any other product that you create, including books, the amount of technology required is truly scalable. If you can get your hands on a decent camera, a microphone, and some standard recording software, you're doing pretty good.

As for software, I've got some good news; a learning management system eliminates the need to have separate software for everything. Recall the multitude of LMS functions I listed earlier. Now, imagine having different software for each of those functions! That would be crazy. A quality LMS is a tremendous help when reducing the complexity of building courses.

Of course, there's quality involved in the technology used to capture and create the content for courses, just like there is for creating any digital product. That quality is scalable from tool to tool across multiple price points. So, it should be no surprise to learn that you can save some money on technology, but that you should think of quality and not only about saving money when investing in the right tools to build your courses.

Let's talk a little about the tools I'm referring to.

For instance, there is recording software in some LMSs. Sometimes that recording software is just for audio; in other instances, it's audio and video.

In some LMSs, you can create quizzes, upload and download PDF documents, create text for your lessons, and embed them directly into the course, all using just the LMS.

Clearly, this is a good thing, as it provides more value for the money you're already spending on the LMS. However, there are many special functions that you may be interested in that an LMS has traditionally not covered.

For example–video capture. You may decide to record videos, and I encourage you to do so for your course material. Video is far more common these days than it was pre-pandemic.

If you had mentioned Zoom as a place to meet in 2018, most people would ask you for directions. Today, Zoom is synonymous with meeting someone virtually over video and audio. You could use tools like Zoom, Microsoft Teams, Loom, or OBS to capture your videos and make them creative. You can even use PowerPoint and Canva to record presentations in creative ways.

Many of the names I listed are common among creators, don't require tremendous investment, and are intuitive to use. I know many of you may cringe when you hear one or two of those names, and that's perfectly fine. You have many options in this world. There will be some tools that you love and some that you hate.

MY GENERAL RULE OF THUMB WITH TOOLS IS TO PICK THE ONES YOU LIKE TO USE THAT PRODUCE THE PRODUCTS YOU WANT TO SHARE.

Other types of tools include software for creating games or interactive video. This market is exploding for online course creators.

As I write this book, some of the more advanced software includes Storyline 360 and Adobe Captivate. These will help you create more interactive video, polished presentations, and more creative lessons with a focus on training applications.

Do you require advanced creative software? Are they too expensive? Are they necessary?

When you first start out, you do not need Storyline 360 or Adobe Captivate to convert your book to a course meaningfully. However, the more features and advanced applications you want for your course, the more you want to look toward software to help you.

For example, you may be comfortable asking questions with a straight up video, and providing a downloadable PDF, or an in-lesson text that asks questions of a learner and allows them to answer in a downloadable workbook. You might have them submit those questions to you through an assignment that is already provided in the learning management system with no emailing files back and forth. Maybe that assignment provides questions that the learner answers for practice, or information they maintain for themselves.

No special software is required. But if you want to increase the interactive nature of the course, and the polished and quality view of your product, then you may decide to fulfill this same learning function using more advanced software like Adobe Captivate or Storyline 360.

Let me give you a little more to think about for stacking technology: the bigger the stack, the more complex the system. As you add more and more software tools, you increase the complexity of your product development and increase the risk of interface problems between software.

I'm not trying to scare you away from using additional software. I'm just letting you know that for every layer you add, you add a layer of potential risk. You need to be smart about choosing software that works well together, has an excellent track record of performance, and is worth its weight in gold.

THIS IS A LESSON ON SPENDING MONEY ON THE RIGHT TOOLS.

IT'S NOT ABOUT BUYING WHATEVER CHEAP TOOLS ARE AVAILABLE ON THE MARKET.

You'll find that most of the bigger software companies have done the work to make their tool reliable and interactive with other software. This is a huge selling point for creators. The student may never know the difference between whether you use a special tool to create that element of your course or not. But you will.

Remember, your learners aren't clients of your software vendors; you are. Those companies want to make you, as the course creator, happy. They design tools to improve your life and the experience you build for your learners. If that's not happening, that company is probably not the right company for you.

Here is a list of additional tools to consider for course creation.

Brillium is software for creating exams. It is a third-party platform you purchase separately from your LMS, but when combined, you can have access to powerful tools to construct exams and evaluate your students' progress.

OBS, short for Open Broadcaster Software, is free downloadable software you can use for video production.

Products like **Restream** or **Stream Yard** are streaming software for live or recorded interview-style lessons. With these, you record an interview with a guest speaker, but it looks like a live stream.

Zoom is familiar to most users and is, therefore, considered trustworthy. You can do all kinds of things with Zoom—like give a presentation—or simply create a solo video.

Loom is great for video capture, especially if you share videos after meetings, want discussions or comments available outside of the LMS, or make simple presentations with or without your image.

Powtoon and **Vyond** are excellent animation software options. Animations can take your course lessons to an entirely new level! I love them.

Consider **Otter.ai** or **Descript** to record and transcribe lessons. Both are excellent tools for developing written content through spoken word. Descript also contains a powerful editing feature across the video, audio, and text elements of a recording.

SELECTING TECH TOOLS

It's important to become familiar with the various technologies available for course creators.

Think about these apps like a user; consider the functions each tech tool provides you. You are buying *functions.*

WE DON'T BUY SOFTWARE TOOLS; WE BUY THE FUNCTIONS PROVIDED BY THESE TOOLS.

For example, you don't buy a lawnmower; you buy the ability to cut grass. You need your grass cut; what tool provides that function? A lawnmower! You want it cut as quickly as possible without having to muscle the mower the entire time. So, you need a mower with a certain blade size and a drive motor. You are buying the ability to cut your grass quickly and easily without hiring a landscaper.

The second purchasing factor is the ease of using or getting that function from that software.

For example, you buy that shiny new lawnmower and learn how to operate it. You open the learner's manual or fire up a helpful YouTube video. You learn how to adjust oil and gas levels, start the mower, adjust the height of the blades, and engage the drive. Now, you can derive value from your purchase by putting it to work for your business.

THE VALUE OF THE TOOL IS EQUAL TO THE VALUE OF THE PRODUCTS YOU PRODUCE WITH IT.

The third thing you purchase is how that technology will serve your business and clients.

This value shows up in two ways: how you interact with the tool and how your learner interacts with the tool. Operate the tool to produce a product (e.g., video, animation, fancy text, downloadable PDF, presentation, game). Your learner interacts with the tool, or the product you produce with the tool, to experience your course.

Those are the three primary points of consideration when buying a tech tool.

In summary, when you buy a tool for your course or business, ask yourself these questions:

1. What function do you need the tool to provide?
2. What software can provide that function?
3. How intuitive, user-friendly, or helpful is that tool to you, the course developer?
4. What will your learners experience when they interact with the tool or with an output of the tool?

You'll note that we haven't considered the software price yet. We don't consider price until we've considered those first *critical* factors. Anything that doesn't provide a necessary function, isn't workable for you, and doesn't serve your learner's experience shouldn't land on your pricing radar. Don't worry about the price of tools that don't meet your needs.

Once you've answered those four questions and you deem the software a viable option, look at aspects of price and availability.

If the thought of buying software makes you anxious, fret not, my friend; here are a few tips for your consideration!

Normally, when you buy web-based applications, they provide:

- a one time purchase,
- a monthly subscription, or
- an annual subscription.

A one time purchase with no annual renewal is great because you pay once and have the tool for the life of the product. These opportunities are becoming harder to find as software companies focus on web-based applications and keep customers through annual and monthly subscriptions.

The annual subscription normally requires one purchase for the year, which renews each year. A benefit of an annual subscription is they usually offer a discount because you're paying for the year in one lump sum. Vendors prefer to get their money now rather than later, so they reward you with a discount. Saving money rocks, right?

Whenever I face a web-based software purchase, I almost always consider saving money by buying the annual subscription as my first option. Naturally, there are people who disagree with that approach. I'm one of those users that does a ton of research, takes the free trial, and then decides what to buy. I don't look back after the purchase.

By the time I get to the purchase decision, I've already convinced myself that this is the tool I'm going to use for the next year. I dedicate myself to that, make the purchase, and save some money by paying for the year in one shot at the point of purchase. It's a long game approach.

You may think, *It's just a little money, dude. Don't be such a tight ass.*

Well, I save several thousand dollars each year by paying annually across all my content creation tools. I don't know about you but saving a paycheck's worth of money is a good thing in my book! It's not a fortune, but a good bit of money each time I make this decision.

Let's shift gears to the pros of a monthly subscription. Buying annually can't be a lopsided victory, can it? What are the benefits of a monthly subscription?

Monthly subscriptions can be fantastic if you don't want to commit to twelve months of use. Maybe you find competitively matched software, where the options are so aligned that you can't decide which is best. You can choose a monthly subscription to keep your options open as you get more familiar with the tool.

COURSE DELIVERY FORMATS

Let's talk a bit about delivery formats. You've picked your learning management system. You've gotten into the software and are familiar with the draft outline of your course. Your book has been an integral part of structuring and creating your curriculum. But now you need to think about how you're going to deliver that curriculum to your students.

Hopefully, you're not asking yourself, "Well, what the heck does that mean? I thought you said we're going to do this online."

Well, that's true. There are several ways to deliver a course online. The first is completely online, self-paced, on-demand learning. In this approach, the student logs into your learning management system and accesses a course with nearly no interaction with you. There is no live content. That student will progress through a logical flow of lessons assembled, recorded, and posted in the learning management system. It's self-paced because there's no instructor there to guide the student. Your video or audio over text will do that throughout the course.

Another method is live online training, where you schedule an event in or out of the learning management system. You can do this inside many of the learning management systems.

In this approach, the students meet you at a set date and time over some form of video streaming software, such as Zoom, Microsoft Teams, Loom, or whatever video software you prefer to use for live presentations.

A hybrid course provides a mix of the fully online self-paced and the live course approach. A hybrid course allows you to mix the two mediums. You may choose to have a live component every week. Between those live question-and-answer sessions, or live lecture sessions where you deliver a structured curriculum, you may provide the student with a mix of self-paced lessons and other reading and audio material.

This reduces the time the instructor must be present with the students. It also gives the students the flexibility to complete a lot of the work on their schedule when it's convenient for them, while also benefiting from live interaction with the instructor at scheduled times.

The hybrid approach is especially effective for coaching programs where you may have a live coaching session with a client once a week, and between those sessions, the student goes through a progression of curriculum inside the learning management system that contains fully recorded, on-demand material. They may work through videos, audio files, recorded presentations, workbook sections, or downloadable PDF workbooks.

Another way you can use the hybrid approach is by going mostly self-paced, on-demand with the course curriculum, meaning the entire course is in the learning management system in some recorded or published format for the student to use at their discretion. Then you space out the live events like the Q&A sessions to once a month, bi-weekly, bi-monthly, or even quarterly.

This puts more emphasis on the on-demand self-paced coursework and provides just enough live interaction for the student to engage with you at an infrequent, but regularly scheduled time. This is sometimes a more helpful pace than the weekly meetings. It all depends on the topic, structure, and volume of the course material you present in the self-paced, on-demand course.

If you feel like your student would benefit from more frequent interactions with you, then the hybrid with a weekly, or even daily, interaction is probably most appropriate. (I didn't mention daily before because I didn't want to overwhelm you.) But yes, you can create a hybrid where you have a live interaction with students daily.

When you combine the self-paced, on-demand coursework with the interactive sessions, you may have a kickoff in the morning for an hour or thirty minutes, and then cut the students loose to do their recorded and self-paced work throughout the day. Then you might briefly meet up again to review the student's progress and answer questions. You will also discuss the unique elements of the curriculum they reviewed and talk about how they've progressed in their workbooks and personal assignments.

As you can tell, there's a scale of interaction at play. You get to decide how you want to use that scale, and how much interaction you want with the student.

My advice here is to do what's best for the student and design a course approach at a pace that works best for both of you. Yes, that means that you will put both things together: the needs of the student and the needs of the instructor.

If you create a course where learner expectations aren't met, they will become dissatisfied, and you'll have a sales and retention problem on your hands quickly.

If you create a course where the delivery method conflicts with your needs and wants as an instructor, creator, or host of the course, you will also be unhappy. You will struggle to meet your obligations to your students, and this conflict will spill over into the students' observation. It may lead them to feel like they're a burden on you despite having spent money to use the product that you created and presented to them. So, balance is super important here.

Now that you have a grasp of course creation technology and how to apply it to your course, let's create a website to support it!

CHAPTER SIX:

CREATE YOUR SITE

I bet you thought we were done with the tech stuff! Not so fast. After covering the high-level course tech topics of websites and learning management systems, it is time to get more tactical and discuss your website and learning management system content.

COURSE LANDING PAGES

When you want to educate someone about the details of your course and how to enroll, you bring them to what's commonly referred to as a landing page. The course landing page is really the home of your course. This is the one page on your business's website or within your learning management system that describes your course and provides guidance on purchase and enrollment.

I like to think of the landing page like the outside of a desirable city restaurant. You approach the entrance as a hungry human searching for food, undecided about where to eat. You expect to observe several things outside of the front door–the menu posted for your review, a clean and organized entrance, and signs of life inside (lights on, an unlocked door, a busy staff moving about)—the amazing smell of food is pulling you closer.

All you must do is convince yourself that this restaurant has a menu you'll enjoy, and it won't take a second mortgage on your house to settle the bill.

Sound about right? Good! Consider your course's landing page in this same context.

The landing page is where students gather all the details about your course before enrolling. Landing pages serve as a door to gain entry to your course. It's where you convince learners that your course contains the solution to a problem they have.

Normally, the landing page contains sales copy and all the good stuff from the back cover of your book, and your product detail page on Amazon. We want to learn a few key things on the course landing page.

What is the course title?

- Who is the instructor?
- What is in the curriculum outline or table of contents?
- How does the course flow?
- Are other items such as workbooks, live question-and-answer sessions, games, templates, or one-on-one sessions included in the course?

Listing these items tells your prospective learner that there is far more value in this course than they initially expected.

They can't possibly turn away from this opportunity, right? *Right.*

The landing page is also your opportunity to make an introduction via a video or captivating pictures. The idea is to draw in prospective learners, show undeniable value, and make them comfortable with you and the course.

Since you aren't there to speak for them in person, this page does the speaking for you. The page is an integral component in building the "know, like, and trust" factors with your prospect.

The landing page gives you prime real estate to focus on the learner, their problem, and a solution.

Don't move from this page without fully grasping this!

The landing page is *always about the client,* their problem, and your solution. It's not a running webpage where you brag endlessly about your bio and the features of your course. You do some of that, but the proper focus is on the learner's problem and how your course helps them solve that problem.

Let's unpack this a bit, shall we?

Describe your ideal learner so they can identify as a fit for your course. You made this course for them, and there is no mistaking that they are the ideal candidate for this opportunity.

Use a structured approach to addressing the problem and solution–use PAS. PAS is an acronym for **P**roblem, **A**gitation, and **S**olution. It is a very popular and effective approach to marketing solutions to people's problems. Your course solves a learner's problem.

This acronym guides content writers and salespeople through a very loose framework to evoke an emotional response from potential buyers. Let's look at each of these individually.

Problem. Describe the problem burdening your potential learner in undeniable clarity and detail. This is powerful for two reasons. The learner sees their problem clearly, and they see you understand that problem. You may help them solve that problem! Use your creative writing skills here without getting too crazy. It must be completely believable and relatable.

Agitation. Explain how that problem creates difficulty for the learner. Take that problem and unpack the negative effects it has on your potential buyer. At this point, the person shopping on your site is caught up in their emotions about the problem and how it *really* makes things difficult for them. They want a solution, and that's what you're going to give them next.

Solution. Explain exactly how your course will solve their problem. This is not an opportunity to brag about your course's shiny, innovative features. This is an opportunity to describe how life will improve after the learning experience. Once the learner has completed your course, it will equip them to: _______________ (insert life-altering benefits here).

Again, don't make the common mistake of droning endlessly about the features of your course. I know you are proud of the course you built! I'll be the first to tell you that you should brag without hesitation about how much work you poured into every detail of the course. However, this isn't the time and place. Save it for the phone call with Mom or your best friend. (You have called them recently, haven't you?)

Learners don't buy features; they buy solutions. Don't get me wrong, people like features! Features may push them over the edge and convince them that your course is better than a competitor's. However, we must convince them to approach the edge before they can go over it. You *must* convince them that your course will help them.

Solutions first; features second.

I hope you can appreciate why website copy is so critical. It's part of marketing, but it's also a part of sales. When you market the course, you get the word out about the course. Often, people find your course through web searches and not a marketing event.

When they find your course through a web search, or a link on a newsletter, podcast, or social media post, they land on … well, the landing page. The page will do the job of selling your course in your absence. When you require a call or appointment to screen and enroll students, the landing page will convince them to contact you, setting the path to a sale.

This is powerful stuff, eh? You can see why it's so important to get the landing page right.

Now that you understand the marketing aspect of the landing page, let's discuss a bit about how the landing page serves your sales process.

You've convinced the learner that your course is a good fit for them, and they decide to move forward with a purchase. Fan-flipping-tastic! Where do they sign up?

Normally, you would include at least one enrollment or purchase link as a button. Yes, that little oval or square block on your page that says, "buy here" or "enroll now" with the link to the checkout page is called a button.

You may choose to disclose the price of your course on the landing page or checkout page. I'm a big fan of posting the price on the landing page because I hate being dragged down a path of clicks and endless page copy to buy something. Holding the price back delays my purchase. (At least in my brain, it does.)

For self-paced learning products, if I'm buying and you're not there with me the whole time, I expect to know how much I'm paying for this product without having to call the Pentagon for the secret codes. Be transparent with your buyers; they appreciate the honesty, which contributes to the "trust" part of "know, like, and trust."

If the product or course is a premium priced product over, say, $10,000, then you may exercise some discretion in whether to post the price. But typically, people appreciate the transparency of putting the price on the landing page. Many salespeople will tell you to hold that price back and not post it on the course landing page because people may not fully appreciate the value of the course, and you might need to talk to them to sell it.

I can agree with that argument, but only for high-priced courses. The perception of what's considered *high-priced* depends on many factors, including your industry's norms, your ideal client's expectations and buying behaviors, and your ability to convey the value. Truly, you need to exercise your professional discretion when making this decision.

You know your learner and your ability to sell better than anyone else does. If you insist on talking to someone before enrolling them in your program, set up an enrollment path to facilitate that action. Not posting the price is one way to do that. It forces that person to go straight to a scheduling tool or form that connects you with them to discuss the opportunity. This usually leads to a discovery call or meeting with that person, which is your opportunity to discuss the opportunity and close a sale.

As you'd expect, there are pros and cons to this approach. One con is that you must be involved in every sale. So, if you're the type of person who's trying to automate as much as you can and avoid direct selling as much as possible, then this would be the least desirable route for you. But if you're the type of person who wants to talk to everyone that comes to your program, and you absolutely want the opportunity to close a sale face-to-face, then this is your jam.

One last point on landing pages: The landing page does not have to live on your LMS.

Although an LMS provides a course landing page, you have the option to host the landing page on your business's website. This might be your existing business site where you build a landing page to do all the wonderful things I've mentioned in this chapter. Here, you will connect the LMS to that landing page through links.

LMS WEBSITE BUILDING

Many LMSs offer more than just course hosting. They also offer website hosting, which makes perfect sense. They provide a landing page to be the front door or billboard of your course for access to purchase or attend the course.

Most LMS companies try to make them intuitive. In fact, some companies invest more in making the website element of the LMS a priority.

They view providing this simplified product as a competitive advantage or a sales point because they know that the typical user isn't a web developer. Most users prefer not to have three or four different sites to manage. So, if they can offer you sufficient website capabilities, it will make the LMS more attractive to small businesses, particularly solopreneurs.

When you design a web page in an LMS, you have page type options—homepage landing pages for your courses—sales pages for other products. I purpose my pages for a blog and other free resources where I advertise my podcast, book sales—all the things. In fact, if you've visited any of my sites, you have seen how I use Thinkific for web hosting and for course delivery. That's right, I use my LMS for all of my website services. Pretty cool, huh?

If you haven't checked those out—*Insert announcer voice here*—"Be sure to check out my websites to stay up to speed, and don't forget to sign up for my fancy, free newsletter."

I'm not telling you this to advertise the capabilities of LMSs. I want you to be aware of the competitive advantage for an LMS company to provide you with this service. I suggest you pick an LMS that provides website service. It doesn't mean you have to use it, but it's nice to have when you consider reducing your software stack.

Most LMS companies offer step-by-step website guides. In fact, many of them offer free courses on how to build your web pages, or how to use their website design tools.

Nearly all of them offer articles, step-by-step directions, or descriptions of what each element of their web builder is capable of. A typical website builder in an LMS will include page banners, calls to action, instructor biographies, student reviews or testimonials, and curriculum descriptions. They offer ways to customize your content checklists with icons, uploaded videos and pictures, and the ability to change page colors, font colors, and types. These are all basic features you'd expect of a website builder.

If you are more advanced with website development and you're comfortable coding, many of these learning management systems provide the ability to embed code on pages. However, all of them will update their themes from time to time. And often, a theme update can make whatever custom code you entered on a page inoperable until you update your code. So, just be aware that if you enter a custom code on a web theme that you keep up with the updates.

If you're falling asleep reading this chapter, I don't blame you. I didn't really care about this stuff when I got started either, or I wouldn't have understood half of it. But it's grown into a significant part of my course and site-building business.

And it is a lot of fun. If you're reading this book, you're most likely a creative person and creating a website can be a lot of fun once you get comfortable with the technology. It's just like when you started writing, painting, or playing a musical instrument. It just took some familiarity before the magic happened. Give yourself some time. Be patient and enjoy the process. Get familiar with building pages in your LMS; trust me, it will save you a lot of money and heartache down the road when you can quickly go in and do some of this work yourself.

If you have no plans of managing or building a website on your own, that's perfectly fine. Hire someone else. But I view it as an assurance that your business can run smoothly if you can do this yourself in an emergency.

I've had clients send me an email saying, "Hey, I was on your website, and I noticed a misspelled word." Or that they really liked the page I built for a course, and they want to know the name of the blocks I used in Thinkific. I want to answer those questions quickly or correct that error on my site because it represents my brand to the public.

It's something that my clients care about, therefore; I care about it.

Now I'm going to throw a little something in here for those side hustlers who are wondering if it's worth spending the time to learn how to use the functions of their LMS. You can make substantial money building course pages, and of course, LMS site pages for clients.

I know people who make a living doing that full-time working from home. They have flexible hours and really enjoy their work. It's something to consider if you're looking for another layer of income, or another revenue stream. Just saying!

CUSTOMER RELATIONSHIP MANAGEMENT (CRM) SYSTEMS

Customer relationship management software (CRM) is a digital hub of business information. Think of a CRM as a single site that captures, organizes, and communicates information for an online business.

Where do you find a CRM? Most professional CRMs are standalone online products. Examples include Keap (the artist formerly known as Infusionsoft), ActiveCampaign, Hubspot, Salesforce, Monday Sales CRM, and the list goes on. You have many options; you need to find the right solution for your business, just like when choosing an LMS. Some factors to consider are functions, cost, accessibility, and integration with other software that you use, particularly your LMS.

Because integrating an LMS and CRM is so important to training businesses, many LMSs incorporate the functions of CRMs while attempting to be the one-stop, single-source solution for entrepreneurs in the course creation business. They are targeting more of the "starter" market. Just remember that just like your LMS, certain CRMs are more capable than others and you may want two very capable platforms rather than one mildly capable platform. Here's some simple math to drive this home:

1 (comprehensive LMS) + 1 (comprehensive CRM) = 2 (very capable systems)

Whereas 1 (mildly capable LMS/CRM solution) = 1 (mildly capable system)

I couldn't help myself.

The point is, professional CRMs are comprehensive, professional, standalone systems that exist to be CRMs and CRMs only. If you score enough business from paying clients, you'll benefit from having one.

So, what's the big deal? What does a CRM do and why do you need one?

Well, here's the list o' things that a CRM may offer you:

- Collect, organize, and manage contact data.
    - Name
    - Email address
    - Phone number
    - Web site
    - Company name and physical address
    - What the contact bought
    - Track emails to/from the contact
- A place to distribute marketing emails.
    - Email templates
    - Email authoring/word processing
    - Collect email open rates
    - Collect email link click rates

    - Distribute emails to specific groups
    - Distribute email newsletters
- Build and use email automation flows.
    - Automated email sequences for prospects
    - Automated email sequences for students/clients
- Trigger tasks in workflows (e.g., a new lead responded to your email, schedule a call)
- Text contacts via a business line phone number
- Create and post checkout forms
- Track sales pipelines
- Manage invoices
- Payment processing
- Appointment scheduling tools
- Lead management

Arguably, the most beneficial aspect of the CRM is capturing the information of every lead and client that touches your business. You capture information for every person who comes to your website, signs up for your newsletter, buys your course, or signs up for a free download. Their information is in your LMS and communicated to your CRM once the two connect.

This is extremely beneficial because it happens without your interaction. You can literally capture lead or client information while sleeping! When you awaken, those contacts are in your CRM and organized by tags. Sweet!

Wait, what the heck is a tag? When someone interacts with your website, or LMS meaningfully, your CRM categorizes them according to the event. The contact interacted with your sites in a way you've previously identified as sufficient for a tag.

For example, if a lead visits your website or LMS and signs up for your newsletter, you may want the CRM to apply several tags to them, including:

✓ New Lead

✓ No purchase

✓ Signed up for Awesome Sauce Newsletter

✓ Entered New Lead email automation

The behavior of the new lead may tell you something about them. For example, if you offer a free course or download on your website or LMS, you can capture the lead's first and last name, email address, and phone number.

You can now apply tags to the contact's profile based on what they've done with your business. This new lead has an interest in your free course or download. You can contact them to discuss other ways you can support them.

In my case, I have the CRM automatically apply a tag that says Free Cat Painting Workshop Download or Enrolled in Cat Painting 101 Course.

When you set up automated tags, and the systems communicate the behaviors of contacts, they automatically associate the behaviors with specific tags.

I break my contacts up into Leads, Clients, and Others (automated in Keap).

Leads have the following tags:

- Lead - B2B Consult/Interest
- Lead - Free Analysis Webinar Attendee
- Lead - Free Preview Enrollee
- Lead - Government
- Lead - Keap Interest
- Lead - Marino Training general lead
- Lead - NOT Responding to B2C Pipeline
- Lead - Ripe No Purchase Yet
- Lead - Thinkific & Keap Support Interest

- Lead - Thinkific Interest
- Interest - Marino Training Email List

Clients have the following tags:

- Assessment Client
- Email List Sign Up (form)
- Nurture - Learn Thinkific student (active enrollment)
- Nurture - 100-Day Launch Client
- Nurture - Hourly Consulting Client
- Bundle/Value Pack Purchaser
- Purchaser - Book
- QuickBooks Contact
- Student - Course Complete
- Student - Repeat
- Thinkific Client
- Keap Client
- DropInBlog Standard

These are tags for the "others":

- Marino Training Partner
- Marino Training Affiliate

General tags in my CRM:

- Appointment scheduled: 30/60/90-minute sessions
- Business - Leader
- Business - Admin Point of Contact
- DO NOT BROADCAST (do not email this contact)
- Vendor
- Prime Contractor

And yes, I apply multiple tags to individual contacts. In fact, most contacts have multiple tags.

My CRM also tracks the emails that are sent back and forth to these contacts because my CRM is integrated with my company email and calendar. This is sweet because when people say, "Hey, Lucas! I'm interested in talking to you about this course," or "I'm interested in meeting with you to learn more about the services you provide," I can send them a scheduling link. Then, they can see the open times and dates on my schedule and select a meeting that fits their life best.

Who cares? Why is this helpful? We don't have to bounce five emails back and forth. We've all been there, and we don't enjoy being there.

"Well, are you available on Tuesday?"

"What about two o'clock? Oh, two o'clock doesn't work because you have a cat painting session."

"How about 4 pm? Oh, four doesn't work because you have to pick your mom up from the grocery store."

"What about 10 o'clock that morning?"

"You know what? Tuesday doesn't work. Let's just do Wednesday."

"Oh, Wednesday's your day for travel. Okay, fine. Let's just push it off a week."

What a tremendous waste of time and energy.

Excessive back-and-forth communication is a waste of time, disorganized, and a barrier to moving forward together. The scheduling tool gives people the opportunity to select the time that works best for their schedule without the hassle of multiple emails.

CRMs also help you manage sales pipelines. A sales pipeline is a step-by-step journey a client takes through your sales process. This normally starts when the lead realizes who you are, interacts with your website or email, and eventually purchases a product.

Sales pipelines are very helpful when tracking clients in a direct sales model where you contact people and work with them one-on-one in the sales process. The pipeline helps you organize where the lead is in your process, how much the opportunity is worth if it closes (sales price), and the time between each phase of the process.

The CRM is also very helpful for tracking meaningful and actionable metrics. On the CRM dashboard, I can see the number of leads I've generated, clients I've served, and contacts I've gathered in the last thirty days. It also shows me if I'm trending upward or downward in these areas over the last month.

This function helps me understand whether things are getting busier or slower. Am I getting more contacts or fewer contacts over the last thirty days? While these numbers aren't a direct indicator of success, they are a decent indicator of meaningful traffic in and out of my business. These numbers do not account for the time I spend on individual projects and how busy I am. Sometimes, gathering less contact over those periods is a blessing because I'm fully consumed with client work (a good problem to have!).

CRM automations are especially helpful for managing email. If a lead or client is engaged in email automation, they will receive a series of personalized emails from me that are preloaded in the system. Just because you have automation doesn't mean it has to be cold and salesy. You should structure emails and automation for very natural communication. You're just allowing the system to send it without you having to press "send."

I use a sequence of emails for free previews and free downloads that allow me to send communications to those clients or leads without harassing or imposing on them. In fact, the automation immediately stops if the person responds. For example, if they respond to the first email asking if they're enjoying their free course or download, the automation stops, and they don't receive the next email that says, "Hey, I haven't heard from you. I just wanted to check in and see how things are going."

As you can see, the website, LMS, and CRM combine to be very powerful for course creators. The only thing more powerful than this combo is the impact of great marketing on your course.

CHAPTER SEVEN:

COURSE MARKETING

Okay course creator, I hope you had fun building your curriculum, website, and learning management system. It is now time to focus on marketing and selling your course.

You designed a course to serve your learners and contribute to your business. To make that happen, you must enroll people in your course. One of the ways to make that happen before fully developing a course is what I call a predevelopment launch.

REDUCE YOUR RISK AND GENERATE INTEREST WITH A PRE-SALE

Let's talk about the anatomy of a predevelopment launch.

I follow a 10-point approach to pre-sales. The first 5 points should be very familiar. I covered them in Chapter Two on curriculum development!

1. **Identify your ideal learner.** Your course serves the learner first, and your business second. You must know who the learner is before you take another step forward. This *may* not be the same profile as your book's ideal reader.
2. **Identify the learner's problem.** What problem does your learner need help with? You must identify the problem before you spend a second developing the solution (course). The problem may be

a performance gap, needed skill, or some other deficiency that affects their life.

3. **Identify and validate the solution.** What solution do you offer to solve the learner's problem? Does it really solve their problem? Are you *sure*?
4. **Identify the learner's outcome.** When the learner solves their problem with your solution, what outcome will the learner achieve?
5. **Identify the value to the learner.** How valuable is the outcome to the learner? If the learner achieves these outcomes, how does it impact their life?
6. **Identify the business fit.** You now have a topic identified and a decent business justification for moving forward. How does this course fit into your business's list of products (Product Ladder)?
7. **Identify learning objectives.** The learner will complete learning objectives as they work through the curriculum. The objectives help the learner achieve the outcome.
8. **Polish the list of learning objectives.** You are almost ready to create content. Before you do, make sure the list of outcomes is tidy. You are going to only build those objectives, nothing more, nothing less.
9. **Finalize the outline.** Now that you have a finalized list of outcomes and objectives, complete a final review of the outline. You now have a much better view of what the course will contain.
10. **Build a landing/sales page.** It's time to make people aware! Build a landing page. It will be the place for potential learners to see your outline, read about the problem and solution, and enroll in your beta group. Payments will be made!

These ten points guide you through a very simple process of identifying the learner, the problem, the solution, the content, and a location to launch.

These ten points do not include building an entire course of content, months of marketing, or a significant investment of time and money.

The reason for this is simple. We need to identify if the course is worth investing in or not.

You'll note that most of the points start with the word *identify. Identify* is not *build.* We are justifying the effort, laying a groundwork for action, and clearing the land to build.

Despite all the obvious benefits of having a course, we don't want to spend a lot of time and money creating a product that no one wants (or buys). Obviously, this is less concerning if you are creating a free course. In that case, you have no aspirations of that course directly contributing to your income or your business.

When you build a course to serve others *and* contribute to your income, you expect a return on your investment. In a pre-sale, the costs of developing a few lessons, a landing page, and marketing materials is the investment. When creating a full course, there is a significant investment, hence there is value in a pre-sale. You'd rather invest less and test the market before going all in.

I prefer to call this a predevelopment launch. We can use a structured approach to gauge interest in our course before we invest time in developing course materials, loading the course in the LMS, and going full-bore on a marketing campaign.

In a predevelopment launch, we promote the course publicly and use feedback and learner interest to decide whether to invest in developing a full course.

This decision becomes more important if you plan to invest significant time and money in filming, script writing, or production services. Courses with those professional elements can run from $20,000 to $100,000, so it's critical to understand whether the customer's need and desire for the course matches your need and desire to create a course.

So, what does a predevelopment launch look like?

First, you'll work through points 1-6 to justify the need for the course and alignment with your business goals. Then, you'll move through 7-9 to finish the curriculum outline. Finally, you'll build a landing or sales page and get the word out.

Remember how a landing page of a course is like a storefront? We're going to build that store's walls and hang the signs. We're just not going to fill the store with all the products.

In a predevelopment launch, we develop the landing page copy, pictures, and calls to action. Visitors to the page will see no difference between this page and one for a developed course.

This is powerful for marketing! You'll be able to share the landing page URL and talk about it on podcasts, social media posts, and discussions. On that landing page, you'll display the outline of the course, including chapter and lesson content and any goals and objectives of the course, including expected outcomes. Remember, people buy outcomes, not features.

So, there's your landing page in all its glory, ready to do all the marketing work.

Behind the scenes in the LMS, you will create and upload a segment of the course. I recommend you start with two chapters of content, the introduction (Chapter 1) and the first chapter of topic-based content (Chapter 2).

Chapter 1 should contain a welcome video, the course outline, and a short starter survey to get to know the client better.

Chapter 2 should contain topic-relevant lessons of valuable content that kick off the course and a working exercise, quiz, or assignment.

That's the bare minimum. You may have anywhere between 10% and 30% of the course developed and loaded into the learning management system, ready to serve your clients for the predevelopment launch.

You also determine if you want to host a discounted offer or sell at full price. I normally launch a beta at a discount of 30-50% off the regular price. In my beta launches, the discounted price provides a tradeoff. The learner pays less money but provides a testimonial and agrees to a drip release of content over multiple weeks rather than having immediate access to all course materials. After the beta, the discount goes away, and learners will have immediate access to all materials immediately upon purchase.

That's all the clean, simple stuff. What about the risky part of the decision to launch before fully developing the course? How many people must enroll before you commit to building the complete course?

You must decide:

1. How many learners must enroll for you to move forward with the development?
2. On what date will you decide whether to move forward with the launch and provide access to course materials?

You must decide how many people you want enrolled before you'll commit to building the rest of the course. If one learner enrolls, will you launch? Do you need more learners before you commit?

You must answer this question for yourself. Consider the price of enrollment, the strength of interest in the course, and the role of this course in your business. You can get fancy and do a breakeven analysis, or you can fly loose and free and ask, "How many people do I need to enroll for me to move forward with development?" That question will drive the analytical minds nuts and make the stick-and-movers happy. In the end, you need to be happy with your decision. It doesn't matter to anyone else.

Naturally, if you offer a predevelopment launch, your potential learners will want to know when they can access the materials.

Be very transparent about this. Tell people you will make the first batch of curriculum available on a specific date. Then, show them the drip release schedule. Include all of this on the landing page.

Be sure to let people know this predevelopment offer is exclusive. You want to create a sense of urgency. After all, you are offering a special price and need commitment sooner rather than later, so you can decide whether to move forward.

The predevelopment launch normally works best if you have a strong following or a loyal group of people that know, like, and trust you. People who are less familiar with you and your products may be more willing to invest in your course after seeing that others know, like, and trust you.

This happens in public or private group settings, like social media groups, so be sure to share the predevelopment launch on your social media.

Offer members of your email list priority access before you announce it to the world on social media. The people on your email list are normally your highest priority because they have willingly entered your circle and have opted into your content. If your social media account disappeared tomorrow, you'd still have your email list to nurture. Always prioritize helping them first.

If your previous customers and clients aren't on your email list, contact them directly and let them know about the course and the amazing discount that you are offering for this limited time.

What happens if you don't have a loyal following to sell to? No worries; everyone starts somewhere. Post those social media posts to whatever audience you have, no matter the size. Send the emails to everyone in your circle, no matter the number of addresses. Get the word out and reward others who will do the same by offering them an affiliate share for any sale that they lead to you.

If you advertise the course over several weeks and you don't get enough interest to satisfy your enrollment quota, either press forward with the people who did enroll or refund their money. Just make sure you contact them individually and notify them of their refund if that's the path you choose. If you proceed with course development, focus on adding new members while serving the enrolled learners. I've done this for as few as two learners and never thought twice about it. Once you commit, stick to your decision, and make the experience great for all involved!

After the start date of the course, you'll need to stay ahead of your students. You may choose to release content on a drip schedule, or you may dedicate the short period leading up to the course to full course development. Either path works if you fulfill your obligations to the learners and provide a quality learning experience.

DISCOUNT COUPONS

Let's talk about discount coupons, which are synonymous with discount codes. You can create and distribute coupon codes to offer learners discounts on purchases in your learning management system. I'm a big fan of coupons. They can help you keep your prices fixed and provide flexibility for discounts and sales incentives without the worry of changing your actual price all the time.

Okay, I hear you saying, "Yeah, dude, I get it. You offer discounts."

But there's a bit more to consider when you develop a coupon in the system, especially if you've never done it before.

You would usually process a discount code or coupon in your learning management system or in your sales site, where you're exchanging funds with a potential course buyer. So, you would have to create a coupon in that system, and that coupon would have a name and display the amount you are discounting.

I like to have fun with my coupon names because I want to make it fun for the user. However, I also make the discount coupon code relevant to the course topic or the person. For example, at EAST Partnership, we sell courses for one of our clients who wanted to offer their course discount to coincide with a big event they were hosting. They were celebrating their fifth year of business, so we introduced the BIRTHDAY CAKE coupon! Who doesn't want cake at a party?

BIRTHDAY CAKE was a series of coupons discounting their courses by 40% and 50%, using two different discount codes. We integrated that into our marketing strategy and called the coupons cake, so on our social media posts, we would say things like—*It's a party; come get your cake.*

We would give a description of the discount and put the discount code on the social media post so the person would enter that discount code, click on the link, and navigate to the course landing page. The course landing page would provide all the information about the course. If they were still interested, they would click on *Enroll Now,* and that button would navigate them to a course checkout page. That is where the discount code would come into play. They could enter BIRTHDAY

CAKE in the discount code block and would realize their discount on the course purchase.

Easy enough. Right? Very clear, easy example. Well, let's look at some intricacies of coupons.

When you establish the coupon in the system, it's not just about having a fun or catchy name. It doesn't have to be fun or catchy. It's not just about naming the coupon. It's also about establishing the right coupon amounts and not overdoing it.

Coupons are best used sparingly and always with a smile on your face. You want to be happy to offer this discount so your regular course price is fair. If you don't price your course in a way that makes you happy and provides the right value to your learners, you won't be happily discounting the price in the future.

I don't use discount codes all the time because it conditions people in your social media network and in your email lists to expect that you're always running a sale and that you will always have a discount later. So, what's the urgency to purchase now? You don't want to condition your network to think that way.

I like to run sales on special occasions and on special occasions only. For example, a course launch, like a beta or pilot, is a good reason to do it. It's fantastic to bring the price down because, in return, you're going to gather constructive feedback from your students. Based on that, you can revise and improve the curriculum. You know, while you're delivering it based on that feedback, and then you might deliver it differently than the final product. It's your first public delivery, so why not offer a discount to get people interested?

Then on the backside, rather than collect the full enrollment fee, you'll collect a discounted enrollment fee. Then you want to gather testimonials and reviews from your students to post on your website. You want to showcase that your students are cheerful people who come to class and LOVE it! It's the best money they've ever spent!

You can use discount codes to chart those untested waters and make those fresh courses attractive to your learners. It also shows them they'll pay more for this later if they don't jump on it now. Everyone likes to be part of something special. It's a bonus if they can save a little money while doing it. So, offering coupons for beta and pilot launches is a good idea.

Special occasions, company birthdays, and major events like summits and conventions are also great for distributing discount coupons.

Again, you're distributing a discount off your regular rate. Set an appropriate rate so you don't feel guilty or hesitant about offering the discount.

Also, make the discount substantial enough to matter. If the coupon offers a small three percent discount on a $100 course, you only saved your client three dollars. That's equivalent to the transaction fee you'll pay PayPal or Stripe. That may mean something to you, but it means very little to your learner. They never see that fee, and three dollars isn't enough to move their needle. So, there is a little psychology at play here.

Offer a discount that's attractive enough, or you're basically wasting your time. It also might make you look a little funny when you're on social media bragging about offering a three percent discount on a $100 course.

Your friends might question whether you're sleeping enough or if you've had your morning coffee. As in most things, there is a need for balance. You don't want to offer too small a discount, but you also do not want to give away the farm by offering too substantial a discount.

You might see people offer steep discounts when they get desperate for sales. They've invested all this time and money into building this product but they're struggling with marketing and sales. They're not getting sales conversions on their site, and they get desperate.

They read an article or see another product being sold at a deep discount, and they're motivated by that. So, they offer a big discount on their course to boost sales (hopefully). They put a ridiculous 70% or 80% discount on the course. Obviously, doing this could have a detrimental effect on how your network views your product's image. They wonder how good your product truly is if you offer such a deep discount.

There'd better be an exceptional circumstance and explained clearly in your marketing copy. "We're offering this once in a lifetime super steep discount." I would avoid offering those big discounts annually; I mentioned before that you will condition your audience. Some people will literally wait to buy your product because they know you offer a discount every year. They'll just wait you out. Don't do that.

This approach also makes people question if you're overcharging for your product regularly. I mean, if you can afford to give it away for a 70% to 80% discount, why are you regularly charging so much for it?

You can see, if you offer extremely steep discounts on your products all the time, it can have some detrimental effects on the perception of your product or brand, or at least your business acumen. Again, let's try to seek some balance.

Create a coupon that seems reasonable. Anything less than ten percent may not get meaningful results. On the flip side, a discount that's too steep could negatively affect your business long term. More than likely, you're going to discount somewhere in the 10% to 40% range. That's your safe space.

Another way you can leverage coupons, and I love doing this, is for bulk sales to increase revenue.

Bulk sales are the sale of multiple course enrollments in one purchase. This may be a company buying ten or twenty seats in your course for their employees or customers.

You can leverage a discount for a certain number of enrollments and use the coupons to provide those discounts to your buyers at checkout. Then you won't have to personalize and send a discounted invoice or walk the buyer through a different checkout process.

I do this often with business-to-business sales. For example, if your company wanted to buy ten seats in my Learn Thinkific course, you could go to my website and see that I offer discount codes on purchases of ten to nineteen students. And you could take that code right off my website and enter it at checkout to save ten percent on that purchase.

I will offer a tiered discount for a larger group of enrollments. A purchase of 20 to 29 seats will receive a 20% discount. An easy-to-remember code that applies to the application of the coupon is ideal. Something like "20-for-20" or "20-seats" works.

AFFILIATE AND REVENUE SHARE PARTNERS

Now let's talk about the potentially powerful relationships we can form with affiliates and revenue share partners.

Affiliates are people who advertise your products, and in return, we reimburse them with a percentage of each sale or a set amount of each sale.

For example, if I were an affiliate for your course, you would provide me with a link to sell your course, and when someone used my link to buy your course, I would automatically earn 20% of that sale as an affiliate or a set fee. We motivate affiliates to promote your products for a profit.

Normally, you choose someone you want to advertise your product, and who will share your links with their network of clients, friends, family, and partners.

And you pay that person to do so when it results in a sale.

How is this different from a revenue partner?

Well, a revenue share partner earns a set amount of revenue from every sale of that product, no matter where it comes from. They don't have to be the seller, affiliate, or have any relationship with the sale. Consider this as being a partner on a product.

When anyone buys your course for any reason, from any location or source, or makes a purchase on your site, you entitle your revenue share partner to a certain share of that sale.

Normally, this is a fixed percentage.

It might be a 50/50 split if you teamed up with somebody to create the course, and you've agreed to split all revenue of the course equally. Sometimes this is a business, host, or instructor relationship. Perhaps you're an instructor and you're paying someone to publish your courses on their learning management system. As the instructor, you earn a revenue share for every sale, and as the host, they earn a revenue share for hosting the course on the LMS.

You can see that affiliates and revenue share partners benefit from partnering with you on the sale of your courses in different ways.

When is one approach more appropriate than the other?

Well, I founded my business on revenue share and affiliate models as a host of multiple course providers.

I have friends who are experts in their fields, and they didn't want to stop what they were doing to choose an LMS and then host and manage courses in the LMS.

They preferred to pay me to handle all that back-end and administrative work and host their courses for them.

In that instance, we established a revenue share model in which I hosted the courses, advertised the courses, and managed the LMS site and administration of the business (e.g., sales, finances, updates, enrollments, and site pages).

They created all the curriculum materials and advertised the courses on their sites and in their circles.

When someone enrolled in a course, we split the revenue according to our revenue share agreement.

Of course, revenue share and profit share are two very different things. Revenue share is just a straight-up split of the total sale. Profit share is a split of the profit after deducting costs.

For example, in a profit share, you would sell a course for $100, and there is a $10 cost (expense) per course. You would subtract the $10 from the $100 revenue and have $90 profit remaining. If you were on a 50/50 share, you would split that $90 profit equally and each of the partners would walk away with $45.

That's a profit share!

In a revenue share, you would sell that same course for $100 and split the revenue 50/50. $50 would go to each partner.

Right about now you should hear a voice in the back of your head asking: *But what about the cost?*

Well, you shared revenue, not profit.

You have a revenue share model. Someone is going to pay for those costs after you split the money, and that's usually whoever the host is.

In that revenue share model, the sale resulted in $50 to each partner, and one of those partners absorbed the $10 cost.

One person walked away with $50 of profit, while the other walked away with $40.

This shows why you must think about how to manage all aspects of the sale and not just the total revenue when developing your agreements and your business model.

I'm a fan of both approaches, depending on the scenario. Sometimes it's better to have a revenue share rather than a profit share. It's cleaner; there's less math involved.

You can set up the ratio to be a little more favorable for the person who incurs the cost. In that situation, maybe the revenue share is a 60/40 split. Sixty percent goes to the person who absorbed the cost, and forty percent to the person without the cost. That approach addresses the cost, and everyone walks away happy without having to do any situational math.

You just set it and forget it from the beginning and review that agreement periodically to ensure everything remains fair.

Next, let's talk about affiliates. It's great to be on both sides of the affiliate coin.

It's fantastic to have affiliates sell your course because they're reaching an audience you may not have access to. Someone actively promotes your courses when you are engaged in other activities (e.g., cat painting). They get the word out about your product, and you reward those people with either a set ratio or a set percentage of the sale or a set fee.

So, we've talked about how those revenue share partners and affiliates can help you. Let's turn this around for a moment and say that you, as a training provider, are also in a prime position to benefit from being an affiliate for others.

For example, I earn affiliate shares from sales of Thinkific accounts, Keap CRM accounts, Wobo digital workbook sales, and DropInBlog sales for my clients. I link each of these products on my website and openly advertise them on my social media pages. I bundle them with the course creation services I provide to my clients. This is a long-game strategy in my business.

The immediate returns may seem small at $24 here, or $38 there, but over time, those numbers grow.

You go from one or two affiliate sales that recur every month to five, then ten, and before you know it, you have fifty or more affiliate sales coming in every month.

In closing, affiliate commissions are a powerful way for you to reward others for marketing your course and for you to earn commissions on the sales of products you use in your business.

Now, let's explore ways to approach sales for different customers.

CHAPTER EIGHT:

COURSE SALES

You learned how to build great curriculum for the right person in the lessons of Chapter Two. But what about sales? Will you sell to the learner or is your buyer another person or organization?

Knowing the ins and outs of different sales approaches may save you a lot of heartache. Let's explore different customer types and ways to approach selling to each.

BUSINESS-TO-CONSUMER, BUSINESS-TO-BUSINESS, OR BOTH?

In this chapter, I'll cover whether to sell B2B, B2C, or both (my preference). Most authors publish a book with the expectation of selling that book to individuals. This is what's commonly referred to as business to consumer, or B2C. When viewed through the lens of a business owner, B2C can be a powerful experience, as the number of potential consumers in a market can be staggering.

However, doesn't selling a whole pile of books to a single buyer sound delicious? Wouldn't you love it if every reader wanted to buy your book for their clients or their staff? This is B2B territory, and it's a wonderful place for book and course sales to live.

B2B, or business-to-business, is extremely powerful for revenue generation. In fact, my business and book writing mentor, Honorée

Corder, focuses much of her energy on helping people understand the impact and opportunity of B2B sales. Let's explore these options in more detail because the approach to marketing and sales is different between the two depending on how you structure your business, how you write, publish, and market your book, and who your course will serve.

When you consider selling B2C, you make your product available and attractive to anyone who may encounter it—particularly your ideal customer, or the client who you intend your book and your course to serve. You need them to know your product exists, and that they have a problem you can solve with that (course, book) product. This is facilitated by the PAS method. You recall that I first talked about this in the section on course landing pages. PAS is an acronym for **P**roblem, **A**gitation, and **S**olution. It is a very popular and effective approach to marketing solutions to people's problems.

In the B2C model, you will sell your course much like you sold your book. People either purchase it through your website or through some other site where you advertise and sell your course. When they click the *enroll in this course* button, they go to a checkout page where they can exchange funds via a credit card or some type of money transaction platform, like Stripe or PayPal. Sweet! You make a sale, and they have immediate access to your course.

This experience is important to your B2C buyer. I encourage you to map out the user's or purchaser's experience, like I just did. What does that experience look like? How did they hear about your product? Where did that information source point them? You may discover that they will find your product in a multitude of places. When possible, they should go to the same place to learn more directly from you–your website and possibly your course landing page. When the customer is ready to make their purchase, they click "buy now" and are directed through the payment process. You'll provide them with login credentials, and the course will be available to them.

The B2B experience is a little different. You need to get the information into the hands of businesses instead of individual consumers. There is a different approach to making them aware that your product exists. You may find it more direct to sell B2B than B2C. Fortunately, direct sales today differ from years past.

I mean, no one wants to wake up every morning to the job of cold calling all day to sell a book or a course. But they have taught those direct sales tactics for decades.

The big difference today is that direct sales happen more often over social media sites and direct messages, instead of door to door. Now it's email to email, or direct message to direct message on a social media platform. That form of direct sales resonates in the B2B market.

Unlike B2Cs, B2Bs are often looking for your solution, and they have money to spend. Often, they're just not aware of your solution because they haven't been reached out to, or they don't know where to look for or find your product.

With B2B sales, you can be direct. And like with B2C, you can have referral sales. Someone you know works at a company and discovers the products and services you offer. They think that would be great for their business and refer your product to people who control money. Love when this happens, and make it happen often.

This brings me to a very important distinction between B2C and B2B. In B2C, the person with the decision-making authority and access to the money is the individual. But in B2B, often, many individuals are involved in decision-making, accessing, and authorizing funds for a purchase. And in B2B, you may open the conversation with one individual and end up closing it with someone else in the business.

It's important in B2B sales to remain aware that your message must reach the person with the decision-making authority. Until you reach that person, either directly or through another person in their organization, you cannot close a sale. And the chances that the right person will just randomly find you and purchase your course are extremely low. So, you need to get into a conversation with the right people, either directly or through a liaison.

This works well for consultants because of the services they sell. They work with a client as a consultant, and if the client wants their team to learn about your topic, the consultant can offer that client several seats in the course in bulk. Bulk ordering is possible on many LMSs but is not on others. So, you need to know that your LMS, or your payment processing system, must be capable of supporting a bulk order. The difference between a bulk order and an individual purchase is that a bulk order is the purchase of many seats for multiple learners in one order. Sometimes bulk orders introduce a level of complexity not experienced by the B2C clients who normally pay with a credit or debit card. We rarely see individual buyers paying with a check, money order, or cash these days.

However, in the B2B market or B2G market, (G means federal, state, or local government), it's not uncommon to receive a check in the mail, or to wait awhile for a payment to process.

Many larger organizations have controlled payment processes and processing systems, and it takes a while for your client in that organization to request funding. They must approve and submit the procurement request. Sometime later, they transfer the money to you via a paper check or a digital transfer.

With bulk enrollments, you essentially have two options. You provide the client with the link to purchase in bulk from your site, and they can use a credit card or a payment transferring system. You can also invoice them, and my clients usually prefer this.

Invoicing helps businesses keep their records straight because they can match an invoice with every expense. It helps them keep their bookkeeping straight, and it's often required in their process. They live in that process all day long and sometimes expect you to be aware of that process even though you shouldn't be. Oh, the comedy—I digress.

B2B sales can be very lucrative. I built an entire business on them, but they can also be administratively burdensome, so you need to be aware and accept that, and be intentional about it. In the end, the financial payouts can be very rewarding.

For example, let's say you create a course after publishing a book for teachers. You get the book in the hands of a client who's a teacher, and they think it's wonderful. They find your book for teachers (ever heard of

The Miracle Morning for Teachers? This is an actual case!) to be extremely helpful and inspiring, and they think every teacher in their school system should have a copy of that book.

Rather than ask every schoolteacher to buy a book with their own funds, they request that the school board support a bulk order of your book. Then they find out you offer a course and submit a bulk order for your course as well.

You will provide the school system with an invoice and coordinate the enrollment of the learners. Usually, you will collect the full name and email address of every learner they intend to enroll. They can simply fill out a spreadsheet and return it. This is how I process the bulk sale enrollments. Then after I receive their spreadsheet, I go into the system, and bulk enroll their students in the course.

Remember when I talked about grouping students? This is a perfect opportunity to group your students in a way that benefits you. After enrolling the students in the course, create a group in your LMS and assign each student to the group. I name the group after the business for simplicity.

Let's say it's the Marino Hydropower Station, and I'm enrolling 100 of their employees in my course. (Hecks, yeah!) I will group all 100 of those employees under Marino Hydropower Station in my LMS. This way, I can easily send bulk emails to the group.

If I want to track completion percentages across the group and submit progress reports to their manager, I can easily do so since I organized them as a defined group in the LMS.

Groups can make life much easier and keep your students organized in your database. Two years from now, when you're trying to remember who Joe Schmo Marino is in your database, you'll find they are part of a group. They were one of those bulk order enrollments from Marino Hydropower Station!

You can see that bulk enrollments and student groups are outstanding when put together.

The benefit of bulk enrollments extends beyond just the sheer number of students being enrolled in your programs. Obviously, there's a financial benefit to having that much sales volume.

Often, to reward B2B clients, I'll provide discounts on scale. If they bring me 0 to 9 students, there is no discount. But if they bring me 10 to 19 students, I give them 10% off each enrollment. If they bring me 20 to 29 students, I give them a 20% discount. I keep scaling their discount up to 30% and stop there. So, they can get as much as a 30% discount on each student.

You want to list the course details in your proposal so your client understands the opportunity and benefits you are offering them.

INCLUDED IN THE PROPOSAL:

- An instructor bio with a headshot.
- Outline of the course and format, including how students will access the course.
- Discuss or list how you will support their students.
- Indicate whether you offer management any administrative benefits, such as weekly progress reports.
- State that you are handling the enrollments and the movement of materials.
- You also want to state clearly if you offer discounts and what those discounts look like at scale.

You know, all the fun stuff.

I want to make one last point on B2B sales: *Referrals are King!*

Referrals in the B2B world are like the *King on steroids*. If you thought one-to-one B2C referrals were amazing, think about how powerful they can be in the B2B market.

There are a few ways that these can materialize from a client within a business. A business takes your courses–they think they're amazing–and they brag about the course in the management meeting that week. Then, the other departments in the organization become interested in your training. That's an internal referral within a client's business.

Then there are happy customers at one organization, referring your product to other happy customers in another organization. Right? So let's say there's a convention in town, and one company has enrolled a bunch of their employees in your courses. Of course, they've had nothing but splendid success.

At the conference, that happy business brags about you to a bunch of their friends who are business professionals at other companies. Before you know it, the second company is taking your course and bragging about their experience to another business. That's business to business, bragging about business to business!

Now that you've seen the power of marketing and sales, it's time to put your courses to work for you. Get out there and move that course!

Along the way, don't forget that, like any other physical or digital asset, maintenance is important.

CHAPTER NINE:

MAINTAIN AND MONETIZE YOUR PRODUCT LINE

My mentor, friend, and co-founder of the Empire Builder's Masterclass (www.empirebuildersmasterclass.com), Honorée Corder, likes to say, "A book in motion is money in motion. A book at rest is money at rest."

Simple wisdom; I love it. And it's a bit of a play on physics, so you know that makes this engineer happy.

Honorée is talking about marketing your book. The same rules apply to marketing your course. Let's rephrase Honorée's awesomeness and see it for ourselves:

A COURSE IN MOTION IS MONEY IN MOTION. A COURSE AT REST IS MONEY AT REST.

-LUCAS MARINO

Let that sink in for a moment. You *must* market your course. And since I dedicate this book to authors of books creating complementary courses, you must market both products effectively to get the most out of the product line. The approach is simple:

BUILD A GREAT PRODUCT + MAINTAIN A GREAT PRODUCT + MARKET A GREAT PRODUCT = OPPORTUNITY

You must also keep your products current and relevant. It's hard to market and sell something out-of-date. Bought expired milk lately? Would you? Of course not!

YOUR COURSE IS NOW A LIVING THING

The product development phase is now over. Enter the product sustainment phase. What is sustainment? Merriam-Webster defines sustainment as "the act of sustaining: MAINTENANCE, SUPPORT." Did I mention that I'm a life cycle engineer specializing in sustainability?

Simply put, you *must* sustain (maintain and support) your products so they can support your clients and your income.

Let's dive in.

BOOK AND COURSE REVISIONS

Once you publish your book, you may make minor updates or revisions to the text in the future. However, you won't edit and release a revision or new edition of your book for one simple typo, the addition of minor content, or a dislike for phrasing. A book requires much more change than that before a new edition is justified. Your course is a living thing you can easily update to keep relevant.

You don't require a publisher's permission or a benefit/cost analysis. There is no golden rule like: "You must update 30% of the course content before a revision is justified." You are the sole decision maker in the course revision, and it can be as easy as creating fresh content, logging into your LMS, and updating lessons. It's not a heavy lift to update text or upload a new PDF or video lesson. It will take you longer to create the updated content than it will to update the material in the LMS.

People know this and expect you'll keep your course up to date. Nurture and maintain your course and it will stay relevant. Relevance gives the course the power to support you. Relevant courses sell.

Maintaining your course over the long run may seem like a lot of work if you try to tackle all updates in one major revision. The idea is to implement updates in small, manageable chunks of work. I have a course in the Thinkific LMS called (drum roll!) ... Learn Thinkific! Genius title, right? *Use the code READER to get 20% off of my Learn Thinkific! course. See what I did there? #coupon*

Many content creators would tell you I'm crazy for creating a course about software that's constantly changing. That didn't intimidate me at all. I know that within an hour, I can learn everything about the new update, and within another hour, produce and post an updated video lesson. In fact, because I'm willing to do that, I assure my leads and students that they have the most relevant course on Thinkific available.

When you take care of the course and complete updates in manageable chunks, you have a healthy relationship with your course material.

For those of you who fear relationships, fear not. This relationship gives back.

When you update small segments of your course, you don't need to go on a huge marketing campaign. A simple update to your course landing page, an email to your audience, and a social media post are good enough. Again, keep a change log to show students what's changed in the course.

Last, keep the course landing page and copy relevant because it's what attracts people to your course and converts sales. Maintaining a sharp and relevant landing page is arguably more important than updating nitpicky little things inside the course. Those nitpicky things, while important, don't sell the course. It's hard to improve someone's experience if they never buy the experience. Focus on keeping your landing page current and relevant, truthful, and interesting.

Now, about those nitpicky details. If that headshot of you from your cousin's wedding in 1992 is still your instructor bio picture, the time is right for an update now that you've completed the course and have less on your work list. If the images you use in your course aren't quite up-to-speed (e.g., a little blurry, not properly referenced, repeated too many times through the lessons, or simply out of date), now is the time to upload new pictures.

Do the things that are necessary to improve the quality and value of your course. Don't shrug them off. Make those incremental improvements. It really will help.

Now, an element that is critical yet often overlooked. When you were developing your course, you were working in the weeds. You had your eyes on the details, and it may have been hard to step back and see the course in its entirety. I'm sure you built a very fine product. But now I want you to look for a very important, and often missing, element. That element is—you.

I don't mean strictly videos and images of you; I'm talking about your likeness *and* your personality. When people create their first course, they often withhold some of their personality from the product because they're focused on being professional, clean, and calculated.

I always recommend you inject personality into the course during the first round of creation. However, if you didn't quite meet that aim, you have the opportunity once the course is live, and you see it in all its glory.

Inject your personality into the course in a way that is fun, professional, and not distracting.

Hopefully, you've seen that effort in this book.

You may love or hate the cat jokes and analogies in this book. But I did my best to weave in my personality, and add a bit of entertainment into this book. I care. And you will remember it, won't you?

It also shows people that you're a person they want to be around. You're the type of person they want to buy more products from. Your learners get to experience you through your products.

They get to know you through your course. They learn about you and experience a bit of your world and your passions without you being physically present. The live Question & Answer sessions and live Ask Me Anything sessions are a fun and natural way to introduce a more personal and relatable touch to your courses.

I encourage you if, at a minimum, you host the curriculum strictly on-demand, occasionally hold a live video conference or meeting with your students, address their questions, and rally around your topic. Again, one way to do this consistently is through an online community.

Don't be afraid to inject your personality into your course in the development phase and after publication. Continuous improvement is the name of the game.

CREATIVE BUNDLING

Your book and course are out there, and together, they're generating income for your business. I encourage you to be creative with bundling your products to the benefit of your learners and your bank account.

You can sell the course as a package deal to increase the quality of your offers to clients. Consider bundling your course and your book as a package deal.

If you offer coaching or consulting services, consider bundling your course and live coaching sessions.

You can even use your book as the pot sweetener for your course by giving a book to every one of your paying learners. The offer would go something like, "Enroll in the course and receive your free copy of my bestselling book, *The Scars I Carry–The true story of a man who misunderstood the title of a course about painting cats and paid dearly.*" Something like that.

For lower-priced courses, you can offer a downloadable eBook version. For higher-priced courses, you could offer both a downloadable eBook and a shipped print copy for learners on the same continent. Something like that.

Offering bundles is much more workable if you've priced everything appropriately, and you have a healthy relationship with the quality of your products and your ability to sell them.

Get creative! Bundle products while selling them individually and always lean toward providing as much value to the customer as possible.

CHAPTER TEN:

FINAL TAKEAWAYS FOR SUCCESS

Let's wrap this thing up, shall we? I hope this book has met your expectations. I strive to practice what I preach about being informative and helping clients close performance gaps. I hope the lessons in this book will give you the knowledge and confidence to kick all the course creation butts and take names (in a CRM, of course).

We started by learning that you *can* create a course. You have the intelligence and the resources. All you need to do is commit, just like when you wrote your book. We talked about your familiarity with the process of course development because of your experience creating and launching your own book.

We also covered several similarities in books and courses, particularly the visual aspects of your course landing page.

We also talked about these chief points in course development:

- Identify your ideal learner.
- Identify a problem you can solve for the learner.
- Identify the outcomes they expect from the course.
- Identify the objectives they must meet to achieve those outcomes.

- Create content that provides an opportunity for practice. This helps the learner complete their objectives and achieve their outcomes.
- Create the basic structure of a course, organizing it into chapters and lessons.
- Assess lesson types and their pros and cons.
- Determine how to assess the performance of your students.
- Determine how to format and deliver the course in a way that meets the needs of both you and the learner.
- Consider methods for delivering and maintaining your online course.
- Understand the importance of developing a marketing plan.

You'll want to grab the *Monetize Your Book with a Course Guide* to make implementing everything in this book that much easier!

It is now time for you to get started. Let's put what we've learned into practice.

I WANT YOU TO TAKE THIS BOOK AND DO SOMETHING GREAT WITH IT: CREATE AN AMAZING COURSE FOR YOUR CLIENTS, ONE THAT BRINGS REVENUE TO YOUR BUSINESS.

Build habits, not reactions. Habits build confidence and intentional success. You saw it in action when you wrote your book. Without intentional, structured work, it is hard to succeed at a high level.

You are more confident when your habits support your success. Reduce the uncertainty in your course development process by dedicating time on your schedule to do it right and do it often. Think of it like your daily writing habit.

My general rule of thumb is that one hour of coursework normally requires three hours of development. The more production you add (e.g., animations, professional videography, scriptwriting, soundtrack production), the more time required. Be careful not to underestimate the time investment added for each new feature you take on. Ever wonder why professional films end up taking years to produce a 90-minute movie? More features = longer production.

I will make you a promise right now—*Your course will not create itself.* You must act, knowing that *you can create a course* and that your learners will benefit from completing your course.

Remove any doubt that you can do this. You won't regret it if you keep your learner at the top of your list of priorities, focus on creating a high-quality course, but never at the cost of creating a perfect course, which obviously does not exist.

The world needs what you have! If it was important enough for you to write a book, it's important enough for you to create a course.

Go out there and serve your community. Help your people and make sure that you send me a note and tell me all about how it went. I can't wait to hear about where this journey takes you.

AUTHOR'S NOTES

Thank you for reading this book!

There is no greater purpose in life than serving others. We can choose to serve in many ways. I served in the military for 21 years. Now, I serve as an entrepreneur.

Entrepreneurship is among the greatest challenges of my life. I suppose you could say that the military prepared me very well for it. In the military, they always prepared me for change. I was prepared for the risk, and I was prepared to lead and understand threats and hard work. They also prepared me for periods of comfort, followed by periods of extreme discomfort.

All of this resonates with the entrepreneur in an unfamiliar environment, under different conditions, and with different risks. It's a hard road, but my career in the military and my time as an entrepreneur have both been very rewarding.

When I left the military, I swore to myself that I'd never work for someone else again. Now, that's a ridiculous promise to make to oneself, but I was convicted in my aspirations of becoming a business owner. I knew that if I was half in, half out, or wishy-washy about owning a business, the result would be abysmal.

Owning a small business is an all-in kind of thing. Half-assing it will not get you where you need to be. You can do the part-time gig to get started. Eventually, if you invest enough and you do it right, this thing is going to take off, or at least get big enough to fully consume your professional energy, and you're going to either take it on or abandon it.

Failure was never an option in my mind. Abandonment wasn't an option either. That meant I had to be convicted of winning the freedom I so deeply desired.

My motivation to be the master of my domain wasn't because I hated taking orders in the military. I had no problem with taking orders and loved serving good leaders. That was one of the better parts of my military experience.

However, it's very liberating knowing that you don't have to ask someone if you can take the day off, allocate the organization's resources, or if you can change what you're working on or who you're working with. There's beauty in having the freedom to make those decisions for yourself as an entrepreneur, especially if you've had a strong background in management.

A lot of that was just because I had spent so long in the military that I was itching as a creative to get out of that space and do something that scratched my entrepreneurial itch. Back in 2019, when I officially retired from the military, my plan was to get a good job, pay the bills, and launch a company. And if the company succeeded, then great! I would be disappointed if the company failed, but at least I had a good job to fall back on.

I suppose I wasn't really prepared for the fun of entrepreneurship, and I am sure I wasn't prepared for the workload required to work at a full-time job and launch a successful training company at the same time.

Although they're very different experiences and environments, they were highly rewarding, and I'm grateful for the opportunity to do both at a high level.

For us to really understand what we bring to others, we must understand what our business brings to us. Occasionally, we must look inward to verify that what we set out to do is truly working well in our lives; that the work we do as entrepreneurs serves others as much as it serves us. And that's not a selfish thing to do.

It took me four years to develop my little single-member LLC to a successful group of multiple brands. I started at ground level and worked my way through, step by step (I purchased the business license over a weekend and made the logo using Microsoft PowerPoint at midnight on a Wednesday). Years later, I have a thriving business. I learned a tremendous amount about myself and about business along the way.

I am passionate about continuing to share my knowledge and expertise with as many people as I can in my lifetime.

It has been my extreme honor to share some of these things with you here, on these pages!

QUICK FAVOR

Thank you so much for dedicating your time to reading this book! May I ask a quick favor?

Will you please take a moment to leave a review on Amazon, Goodreads, or where you purchased the book? Your words have power. Your review can help this book serve more people. I appreciate you!

GRATITUDE

To my wife and best friend, Tammie. You are the greatest woman I've ever met, and I thank God every day that you chose me as your husband. Thank you for leading our family for the past twenty years. You've been a military spouse, a mother, and the wife of a high-energy entrepreneur that often doesn't know how to say "no." Without your support with EVERYTHING, the kids, family, and friends, I wouldn't have been able to build our livelihood, let alone this book. I love you, Tammie.

To my kids, Caleb, Gabriel, and Madelyn. I love you more than you'll ever know. My life was incomplete without you. Each of you is uniquely YOU. Keep it that way, you are amazing humans. Make good decisions!

To my parents, Charles and Barbara. Thank you for buying all those books when I was a quiet kid. I honestly cannot imagine who I would be today if I didn't latch onto books as a child. I was perfectly content with my latest read and the world you built for me. You always encouraged me, regardless of how farfetched my ideas may have been. Oh, and thanks for having my back that one time in high school English class. That was a damn fine piece of creative writing if I do say so myself.

To the all-star team of writing and publishing excellence: Honorée Corder, Karen Hunsanger, Dino Marino, Terry Stafford, and Brian Meeks—you rock! You took this book to another level!

Karen—you were my trusty sidekick, voice of reason, quality assurance team, and talent manager all-in-one throughout this project. Without your energy, this book would be a fraction of what it is. THANK YOU!

Honorée—you were my mentor, coach, confidant, and source of motivation when I needed a shot of inspiration or a shove in the right direction. I am blessed with your friendship and guidance. Thank you for sharing your wisdom with me!

Get a comprehensive education in online course creation, marketing, and business with these courses at www.marinotraining.com

If you are looking for an online community of creative entrepreneurs, consider the Empire Builder's Masterclass. We offer something for every creative entrepreneur including an online community, blogs, videos, and courses to help you build your books, courses, mindset, business, and more!

Learn more at www.empirebuildersmasterclass.com

WHO IS LUCAS MARINO?

Dr. Lucas C. Marino, D.Eng., PMP is the founder and owner of Marino Consulting Services, LLC and his two training companies, Marino Training and EAST Partnership. He is also co-founder of the Empire Builder's Masterclass, a training resource for creative entrepreneurs.

Lucas helps entrepreneurs and authors launch and sustain online training products. Lucas is a Certified Thinkific Expert and host of the Conversations with Course Creators podcast.

A military engineer by experience, he spent 21 years as a naval engineer in the United States Coast Guard. He then founded Marino Consulting Services, LLC, and worked in several senior Logistics Engineering Program Manager roles for military acquisitions, including Army landing craft and the Navy's COLUMBIA submarine program. Then he decided the time was right to realize his dream of being a creative entrepreneur, and he made the big leap!

He received his MS in Systems Engineering and Doctor of Engineering degrees from The George Washington University.

Lucas has a passion for developing others and partnering with other entrepreneurs! He also loves cats and wants everyone to know, including Mr. Pickles, that no cats were harmed in the writing of this book or in the development of any course, course material, or any other thing having to do with books or courses.

Marino Training

Email: lucas@marinotraining.com

Marino Training: www.marinotraining.com

Empire Builder's Masterclass:

https://www.empirebuildersmasterclass.com/

LinkedIn:

https://www.linkedin.com/in/lucas-marino-deng/

LinkedIn Company Page:

https://www.linkedin.com/company/marino-training/

Twitter:

https://twitter.com/marino_training

Facebook Page:

https://www.facebook.com/marinotraining

Facebook Private Group:

https://www.facebook.com/groups/monetizeyourbookwithacourse/

Made in the USA
Middletown, DE
28 February 2023